THE IRISH SENATE

THE IRISH SENATE

by Thomas Garvin

Research Series: 1

INSTITUTE OF PUBLIC ADMINISTRATION
57-61 LANSDOWNE ROAD, DUBLIN 4

PUBLISHED BY THE
INSTITUTE OF PUBLIC ADMINISTRATION
57-61 LANSDOWNE ROAD
DUBLIN 4

First published 1969

Printed by Mount Salus Press Ltd., Sandymount, Dublin

ACKNOWLEDGMENTS

The bulk of the material contained in this essay was collected for an M.A. thesis in Politics which I completed in late 1966 under the supervision of Mr John Whyte, Department of Ethics and Politics, University College, Dublin. I would like to thank Mr Whyte for his guidance and encouragement. I would also like to thank the various public representatives and others who would probably prefer to remain anonymous, who gave me so much of their time. Mr Desmond Roche, Principal of the School of Public Administration, helped me a great deal more than he realises. Thanks are also due to Professor Basil Chubb, Department of Politics, Trinity College, Dublin, for much courtesy and assistance. Lastly, I would like to thank Professor Conor Martin, Department of Ethics and Politics, University College, Dublin, for his unceasing support and encouragement.

T.G.

CONTENTS

Chapter One

THE SECOND CHAMBER
IN IRELAND
1920 - 1936

1. FOUNDATION, COMPOSITION AND CAREER

In 1937 the Irish Free State was disestablished in favour of a
new semi-republican constitution. No radical changes were
made in the mechanics of Government — the nomenclature was
changed, the theory of sovereignty was new, but the functions
and inter-relationships of organs of State remained fundamentally the same. In particular, the supremacy of the Dail and of
the Cabinet was not rivalled, as it had been until mid-1936, by
a strong Second House in the legislature. The new constitution,
however, did provide for a Second Chamber of the same size as
its predecessor, bearing the same official title — Seanad Eireann
— and designed to replace the Senate abolished in 1936.

Despite its outward similarity to its predecessor in function
and even in personnel, the new Senate was to have a very
dissimilar history, have different functions and objectives and
a rather different role in parliamentary and national affairs. Its
constitution owed a considerable amount to the lessons of the
experience that had been gained with its predecessor, and to
understand the new House it is necessary to see it in the perspective of the history of the Senate of the Irish Free State.

This House had had a short and chequered career, having
included in its membership some of the best-known public figures
of the time and having taken an active, independent and
effective part in public affairs which was to be contrasted with
the rather minor role which its successor was to play. Its
composition and powers had been devised according to what
might now be considered a rather conservative conception of
what a Second Chamber should be and do, and these features
were fated to be tested by political conflicts of a particularly
stormy character. These characteristics, their part in determining the subsequent unfortunate history of the House, the
demands of cabinet government and the peculiarly Irish condi-

1

tions which led to the decisions to abolish it and replace it with a semi-vocational electoral system for the new Chamber, affected decisively the functions and powers given to the new Senate by the Constitution of 1937.

There was strong British and Unionist support for the inclusion of a Second Chamber in the 1922 Constitution of the Irish Free State. Griffith wrote to Mr Eamon de Valera in November 1921 reporting a meeting in London he had had with leaders of the "Southern Unionists". He said that they had urged that there should be a Senate included in the Constitution, that he had agreed in principle and had promised that they would be consulted when the time came to decide how the House should be constituted.[1] The idea of a bicameral Irish Parliament was not new, as the Westminster Home Rule Acts of 1914 and 1920 had included schemes for a Second Chamber. The Government of Ireland Act, 1914 provided for a Senate of forty members serving for fixed terms of five years, elections to be from constituencies based on the traditional provinces. The Irish Convention of 1917, held as a conservative counterblast to Sinn Fein, proposed a somewhat similar scheme.[2] The Government of Ireland Act, 1920, which superseded the 1914 Act and which was to be superseded in turn, as far as "Southern Ireland" was concerned, provided for a Second Chamber consisting of three ex-officio members, seventeen crown nominees and forty-four elected members representing the Catholic Church, the Church of Ireland, the Irish peerage, the Privy Council and the local authorities.[3] Elections to this House were actually held in 1920 at the same time as the elections to the Southern Irish Lower House—the latter being regarded by Sinn Fein as being held for the Second Dáil.[4] The Dáil refused to recognise the elections to the Southern Senate because of the power given to the Crown to nominate some members. The Crown's nominees met once for fifteen minutes and then adjourned *sine die.*[5]

Originally, the Senate of the Irish Free State was intended to contain six university members. Kevin O'Higgins caused these seats to be transferred to the Dáil, where they remained

---

[1] As cited by Senator W. Quirke; *Senate Debates* 20: 1896, 16th January 1936, in O'Sullivan, D.: *The Irish Free State and its Senate* (1949), p. 75.
[2] Donaldson, A. G.: *Some Comparative Aspects of Irish Law* (1957), p.p. 69, 72.
[3] *Ibid*, p. 73.
[4] Coogan, T. P.: *Ireland Since the Rising* (1966), p. 31.
[5] *Ibid.*

for most of the lifetime of the Free State, reappearing in the new Senate in 1938.[6] The figure of sixty senators was decided upon because the Unionist spokesman requested it: originally, a House of forty members had been envisaged.[7]

The Unionists also urged that the franchise in senate elections be subject to a high property qualification, but the Government, feeling that there would eventually be strong pressure to democratise such a franchise, finally decided upon an electorate of all citizens above thirty years of age voting in a nation-wide constituency. Senators were required to have attained thirty-five years of age and it was specified that candidates should be proposed

> . . . on the grounds that they have done honour to the Nation by reason of useful public service or that, because of special qualifications or attainments, they represent important aspects of the Nation's life.

Mainly because of its rather general character, this proviso soon became ineffective.[8]

One-fourth of the senators were to retire every three years and be replaced by election. The first House was formed according to special provisions; the President of the Executive Council (Prime Minister) nominated thirty senators, and the Dáil elected the remainder. Of the nominees, eight were peers, four were baronets and one was a Knight; eleven had served in the British Army and thirteen had been educated at English public schools, Oxford, Cambridge or Trinity College, Dublin.[9]

The House's power to delay legislation was used eleven times —eight of them being after 1932, when Fianna Fáil came to power.[10]

Popular election to the Senate was attempted once, in 1925, and was a failure due to lack of public interest. In 1928, the system was changed by means of constitutional amendment. It was provided that one-third, instead of one-fourth, of the senators should retire every three years, thus reducing a senator's maximum term from twelve to nine years. The elec-torate consisted of the members of both Houses of the Oireachtas. The delaying period the House could enforce was increased from 270 days to eighteen months, with two more

---

6 O'Sullivan, D.: *op. cit.* pp. 84, 85.
7 *Ibid*, pp. 77, 78.
8 *Ibid*, p. 86.
9 McCracken: *Representative Government in Ireland*, p. 138.
10 Donaldson, A. G., *op. cit.* p. 151.

months for reconsideration. Its power to demand a popular referendum on legislation was deleted at the same time.

The powers of the House over financial legislation were negligible, as dictated by British precedent and experience.[11]

While its legislative powers were weak and public interest in its activities small, the Senate was able to present a very real threat to non-financial legislation. Needless to say it would have been a very dangerous power for the House to use against a hostile, hurried or determined Dáil, as the constitution could be amended by simple Act of the Oireachtas. Ultimately, the Senate depended on the Dáil's goodwill for its very existence.[12] Ironically, in view of subsequent events, one of the reasons for the deletion of the referendum power from the Constitution was that it was feared that that power might be used some day to alter the constitutional position set up by the Anglo-Irish Treaty.[13]

Class, political and religious minorities, then, were granted political safeguards under the Anglo-Irish agreements, and were the immediate reason for setting up a Senate to work alongside the Dáil in governing the new State: one of its main functions was to oppose discriminatory legislation. The two Houses made strange bedfellows: the post-revolutionary Dáil, even though it lacked anti-treaty representation in its first years, and the explicitly conservative Senate represented differing political viewpoints whose points of contact were sometimes few and rather tenuous.

The amount of revisionary work done by the Senate in its first ten years was considerable.[14] Relations with the Dáil were comparatively amicable, due mainly to the fear, shared by many of the senators and by the Government, of the intentions of the anti-Treatyites who were reforming after their military defeat in the Civil War.

The House had serious weaknesses not immediately evident in its early years. The triennial elections altered the composition and political alignment of the Senate slowly in response to the opinion of the people as reflected in the Dáil, thus making

---

11 Kohn: *The Constitution of the Irish Free State*, pp. 199-201 and Donaldson, A. G., *op. cit.* p. 151.
12 Mansergh, N: *The Irish Free State: its Government and Politics* (1934), p. 140.
13 Kohn, *op. cit.* p. 200.
14 Douglas, J. G.: *Mr. de Valera and the Senate* (1934). Bennett, T. W. W., *Pro Domo Suo* (1934). Mansergh, N., *op. cit.* p. 98; O'Sullivan, D., *op. cit.* appendices.

for a "time-lag" between the two Houses, which was aggravated by the fact that the anti-Treatyites had had little say in the formation of the Senate in 1922. The Senate tended to reflect sets of opinions which were rapidly dated as the new political order in Ireland changed, settled down and established itself.[15] The deletion of the referendum power and of popular election isolated it further, although the shortening of the senators' terms from twelve to nine years might have mitigated the effects of these changes to some small extent had the Senate survived.[16]

The unpredictability of a House in which party influence was weak and in which a large number of independent members held the balance of voting power was certain to irritate the Cabinet: the blurring of party lines, far from being a virtue, was a nuisance as far as the Executive was concerned—a nuisance which would quickly outweigh the advantages of competent revision work if it became too prevalent.

Party lines began to harden in the Senate after the 1928 triennial election. It immediately became apparent that the triennial system had resulted in ensuring a majority in the Senate for the Cumann na nGaedheal Government not only up to the time of that Government's leaving office, but well into the term of office of any other Government as well. Fianna Fáil came to power in 1932, and might have expected to achieve a sympathetic majority in the Senate by 1937, had the House remained in existence that long.[17] The seed of the Senate's destruction lay in the political unbalance that finally resulted from the triennial system of replacement of personnel.

2. THE END OF THE FREE STATE SENATE

The Fianna Fáil Party took its stand on an interpretation of revolutionary legality which dated from the Proclamation of the Irish Republic in 1916 which received its ratification and expression in the "Dáil Constitution" of 1919. The Oireachtas of the Irish Free State was regarded as the result of a *coup d'état;* the signatories of the Anglo-Irish Treaty had by-passed the revolutionary Dáil, it was claimed, and the Dáil of the Irish Free State was therefore illegal. However, by 1927, it was admitted that the Free State Dáil was in some sense a represen-

---

[15] Mansergh, N. *op. cit.* p. 99.
[16] Kohn, *op. cit. p.* 140 *et seq.*
[17] O'Sullivan, *op. cit.* pp. 463, 464.

tative body and it was recognised to be the effective source of political power in the country.

The Senate, however, was outside this pale of toleration. Its conservative character, its obvious "post-British" nature, and the fact that it would determinedly oppose Fianna Fáil even if that party had acquired the mandate of the people increased the probability of an open clash.

Other parties sometimes looked askance at the House too. Cumann na nGaedheal ministers were not unknown to have regarded it as an interloper and as a nuisance.[18] The Labour Party had never been enthusiastic about the Senate although its leader supported bicameralism in principle.

It was, in fact, the Labour Party which first suggested that a Senate composed on a vocational basis would be more appropriate. This idea was later to be taken up by much more right-wing groups.[19] Johnson, the Labour leader, explained his support for such a scheme in 1922 as following on Connolly's belief that some form of vocationalist or syndicalist organisation would be the only way of spreading socialism in Ireland.[20] President Cosgrave approved of the idea, but it was dropped as impracticable.

The idea of special parliamentary representation for interest groups either in a Second House or in a separate "economic parliament" had a brief vogue in Britain in the years following the First World War. Such writers as Barker and Laski were attracted to it for a while, as were the Fabians.[21]

The idea lingered very persistently in Ireland; in 1928, a Joint Committee on the Constitution of Seanad Eireann considered a suggestion to the effect that the Oireachtas should select a nominating panel,

> . . . representative of associations, organisations or bodies representing the following interests, viz., Agriculture, Labour, Education, Commerce and National Development.

The idea was approved, but, once again, no-one could see any way of making it a practicable one, and the Committee finally

---

[18] For Mr de Valera's attitude, *Dáil Debates* 22:140, 22nd February, 1928. For Cumann na nGaedheal, see Moss, W.: *Political Parties in the Irish Free State* (1933), p. 50.

[19] A good example is Mr Frank MacDermot, who envisaged that the vocationalisation of Irish society would result in the elimination of the Labour Party as a "political monstrosity": see *Senate Debates* 21:302, 13th July, 1938.

[20] *Dáil Debates* 1:1141-1144, 25th October, 1922.

[21] Birch, A. J.: *Representative and Responsible Government* (1964), p. 105 *et seq.*

contented itself with an overhaul of the existing machinery. Mr de Valera opposed the vocational suggestion as he had opposed a rather similar proposal in 1922.[22] However, he was opposing the Senate as it was then constituted rather than the idea of vocational organisations: Mary MacSwiney and he had suggested that some such scheme be applied to a reformed, subordinated and weakened Senate in 1926, and Mr Lemass had expressed qualified support for the idea in 1928.[23] It is significant that, in 1922, recognition was given to the basic idea; Dáil Eireann resolved that President Cosgrave, before making his nominations to the Senate, should consult various prominent vocational bodies.[24]

Vocationalism appealed to many of all political persuasions: to the "haves" it seemed to offer protection—special representation for property owners—while to the "have-nots" it seemed to offer a voice, it seemed to be blessed by the writings of James Connolly and it was also seen as a safeguard against an excess of "geographical"—or popular—democracy. Vocationalism was fashionable in Britain and in Germany in the 1920's, and Mussolini and Pius XI were soon to lend support to differing interpretations of the idea. In Ireland, it was looked upon by many as a panacea. There were as many interpretations of it as there were supporters — it appeared to some as a way to revitalise the whole organisation of society, while to others it was merely a method for obtaining expert advice efficiently.

The idea expressed in 1922, 1928 and later was that, without compromising the democratic principles on which the Oireachtas was based, the Second House should be as different as possible from the Dáil in composition and should bring a competence to legislative business which a Lower House, elected according to geographical democracy and consisting mainly of amateurs, could not give.

Following on the recommendations of the 1928 Joint Committee, the terms of the senators were shortened and the Senate's position weakened. In place of popular election, a panel was provided containing twice as many candidates as there were seats in the House to be filled, one-half of this panel being

---

[22] *Dáil Debates* 1:1141-1144, 25th October, 1922 and *Report and Proceedings of the Joint Committee on the Constitution of Seanad Eireann*, 16th May, 1928, Part V, section 2.
[23] *An Phoblacht*, February 1926 *et seq; Dáil Debates* 22:140, 22nd February, 1928.
[24] Bromage, A. W. and M. C.: "The Vocational Senate in Ireland", *American Political Science Review*, Vol. 34, No. 3, June 1940, p. 520.

nominated by each House. The electorate consisted of the members of both Houses, and the final vote was by postal ballot.[25] Parties calculated the number of nominations they made so as to get the maximum number of seats from their available voting strength.[26] However, the House did not alter radically in composition; by the time of Fianna Fáil's entry into office in 1932 the Houses of the Oireachtas were "out of step", and never were to be in step again as long as the Irish Free State lasted.

The last years of the Free State saw an intensified debate on constitutional government; there was widespread dissatisfaction, whether tacit or openly displayed, with the existing system, and schemes for reform or replacement of the institutions of State were common. Even corporativistic schemes for the reorganisation of society on functional "vertical" lines were aired in sections of the reformed Cumann na nGaedheal Party—now renamed the United Ireland or Fine Gael Party.[27] As we have seen, qualified approval of vocationalist ideas—as distinct from approval of a radical reorganisation of society on corporate lines—was expressed in both the Fianna Fáil and Labour Parties. Pius XI had expressed his support for it in his encyclical *Quadragesimo Anno* in 1931.

As applied to the Senate, vocational schemes and suggestions entailed giving the Chamber over to "representatives of production". This would supplement, or even supplant, popular representation in the Lower House, and act, even more effectively than does conventional political democracy acting through mass parties, as a resolver of conflict and as a social coagulant. The theory was simple but the practice was not to prove so simple. The proposals favoured in Ireland had three basic origins : corporativist ideas as developed by Italian fascism, the Papal Encyclical and Fabian developments of the Guild Socialist idea.[28]

Care should be taken not to overrate the affects of political theories or ideologies on Irish politics. In comparison with most European countries, social theories did not have a decisive influence on discussions about governmental machinery. In the end, the mingled traditions of French revolutionary democracy and British parliamentarianism were to determine the shape

25 O'Sullivan, D.: *op. cit.* p. 235.
26 Bromage, A. W. and M. C., *op. cit.* p. 521.
27 *Outline of Policy of Fine Gael* (1934), pp. 12, 13.
28 See Barker, E.: *Principles of Social and Political Theory*, p. 77.

of the Irish Parliament, including the form of the reconstruction of the Senate. The vocationalist ideas were to leave their mark, however, and give rise to an apparent dichotomy between the aims and actual activities of the present House.

Fianna Fáil spokesmen were the most hostile to the Senate. It was criticised for extending protection and political power to a class which had been rejected by the people, for being anti-nationalist and pro-British. Its abolition or radical reform was urged.[29]

In 1933 the party won an overall majority in the Dáil and did not have to depend on Labour support to stay in office. Before the election, the party committed itself to the abolition of the Senate and, while not promising to reconstitute or replace it, it was stated that the number of its members would be reduced if it were decided to replace it.[30]

The Senate amended much of the new government's legislation, more often because of faulty drafting than because of the object of the legislation.[31] It did, however delay the Bill to abolish the Oath of Allegiance to the Crown, requesting the Government to consult the British Government before carrying out a deletion of a provision which was entrenched by the Anglo-Irish agreement of 1921. It also delayed the granting of universal suffrage in local government elections and limited the operation of the Bills keeping the Army in being. The Senate's amendments to the control of Manufacturers Act was criticised bitterly—this Bill was, perhaps, the cornerstone of Mr de Valera's policy of economic autarchy.[32]

The constitutional provisions that were seen by the Government as being the last relics of British imperialism in Ireland were the very ones which the House would try most energetically to protect—those devised as assurances to the Southern Unionists in 1922 as lines for their loyalty and as a basis for a possible *rapprochement* with the North. The Senate itself was, at least in part, one of those provisions, and would be tolerated as long as it did not get in the way. Fianna Fáil senators sat in the House, but their attitude was stated bluntly by one of them:

I say for myself, and I think I can say for every member of this Party, that we came into it (the Senate) on the invita-

---

29 *Dáil Debates* 22 : 140, 22nd February, 1928.
30 O'Sullivan, D., *op. cit.* p. 367.
31 Bennett, T. W. W.: *Pro Domo Suo* (1934).
32 *Dáil Debates* 51 : 1903, 18th April, 1934.

tion of the Party. When I came in here, I came in on the definite understanding that, when the time arose, I was to be here to do my bit to wreck this house . . .[33]

When the Senate rejected a Bill forbidding the wearing of uniforms except by State-authorised organisations—a measure aimed primarily at O'Duffy's semi-fascist Blueshirt organisation—the Government promptly introduced a Bill abolishing the House.[34] Mr de Valera foresaw that the Senate would hamper and possibly frustrate completely his attempts to give legal and constitutional expression to his own ideas concerning the organisation, status and allegiance of the Irish State. He acknowledged that he did not regard the Second Chamber as an essential part of a democratic Parliament; the Senate was a "vestigial remnant of obsolete constitutional arrangements" and the existence of Second Chambers was, historically, largely accidental.[35]

He acknowledged that there was something to be said for the Senate's revisionary work, and hinted that, once a unicameral legislature was established, the Dáil's Standing Orders would be modified so as to allow of a further careful examination of legislation after Report Stage. In the event, however, nothing was done to replace the House's revisionary functions until the new Constitution's Second Chamber went into operation in 1938.[36]

The Abbe Siéyès' classic dilemma, to the effect that, if two Chambers agree then one is superfluous, and, if they disagree, then one of them is pernicious, was discussed at length in the debate on the abolition of the Senate in the Dáil. Cosgrave expressed fears of a long Parliament,[37] while Norton, the Labour leader, roundly condemned the House as having been a "rubber stamp" for the Cosgrave Government.[38] In the Senate, the chairman relinquished his neutrality so as to make a spirited defence of his House, pointing out its positive contribution to legislation and denying that it had acted in a partisan manner.[39] Understandably, the House delayed the Bill. The suspensory period expired on 24th November 1935, but no move was taken

---

[33] As cited by O'Sullivan, D., *op. cit.* p. 516.
[34] *Dáil Debates* 51 : 1828 *et seq.*, 18th April, 1934.
[35] *Ibid*, 1830.
[36] O'Sullivan, D., *op. cit.*, p. 366 and p. 478.
[37] *Dáil Debates* 51 : 1836, 18th April, 1934.
[38] *Ibid*, 1876.
[39] Reprinted as *Pro Domo Suo*.

to abolish the House, which was now defenceless. Mr de Valera stated soon after

> . . . if anyone can indicate to us how to set up a Second Chamber which will serve us and will not be a definite barrier to progress or be simply a reproduction of the conditions in this House, I shall still keep simply an open mind.[40]

The Senate considered the Bill again, and suggested that a Joint Conference be held to discuss how it could be replaced by another Second Chamber on some basis more acceptable to the Government. It seems probable, however, that the Government, realising that a Second Chamber might hinder moves toward a new constitution, wished to get rid of the old House completely before taking any action. The Senate's proposal was ignored, and the Governor-General signed the Bill of Abolition on 29th May, 1936. Thus ended the first essay in modern Irish bicameralism.

The Oireachtas was soon to convert itself into a Constituent Assembly. The 1922 Constitution was now "a thing of shreds and patches", and what remained of it rather resembled the Dáil constitution of 1919—a bare description of the mechanics of assembly government and an apportionment of sovereignty.[41] The way was open for a new essay in constitution building.

A few days after the signing of the Abolition Bill, on the 9th June, 1936, a Commission was appointed to examine the possibilities of setting up a Second Chamber as part of the new Constitution if it were decided to replace the Senate. It reported on the 1st October. Independently proposed schemes for a Second Chamber were common, and there was influential support for such a House: soon after the Commission had been set up, the President of the Association of the Chambers of Commerce appealed for a new Senate, explaining that it was felt that some sort of bicameral system was essential, first "to give that feeling of confidence without which industrial and commercial development is impossible" and also to ensure that legislation which affected industrial and commercial affairs would receive "the consideration necessary for the protection of the commercial community".[42]

Not only the commercial interests supported the idea—the ex-unionists, Fine Gael, sections of the Catholic Church and, in

---

[40] O'Sullivan, D., op. cit. p. 457.

[41] Grogan, V.: "Irish Constitutional Development", Studies, 1951, pp. 383-398.

[42] Irish Independent, 26th June, 1936.

general, conservative groups expressed their desire for a bicameral Parliament. On the other hand, the vast majority of the Fianna Fáil and Labour parties' rank-and-file, and probably most of the population, were apathetic or hostile towards bicameralism.

Bicameralist opinion was also sympathetic toward proposals for a vocationalist Senate. Such a Chamber, it was affirmed, would have a therapeutic effect on party conflict.[43] It was claimed that the House could be made up of representatives of existing organisations, or, alternatively, it could be a mixed House, composed partly by nomination and partly by election, a vocational element being introduced at some stage in the process.[44] Defence of the Constitution should be one of its primary functions, some people believed; geographical democratic representation was not enough, said others.[45] From a stock of ideas such of these was developed the scheme which was finally put into practice.

The Senate of the Irish Free State had always been uncertain of its position. Public apathy towards it, the flexibility of the Dominion Constitution and the scant regard given it by ministers of all parties made the House "somewhat touchy of its dignity". British and Dominion precedents indicated that the Upper House should overshadow the Lower House at least ceremonially. In Ireland, these precedents were never followed: revolutionary tradition, self-conscious democracy and the bitterness of class conflict took even this precedence away from the Senate.[46] Its increasing exclusion from the mainstream of political life resulted in even its supporters remarking its disimprovement during its last years.[47] Competition between the parties for seats caused its composition to wander further and further from what the intentions of its founders had been. As the Dáil tended to contain a broader spectrum of political views and groups, the Senate became a political football.[48]

Its alienation became so complete that when it rejected a Bill

[43] Binchy: "Proposals for a New Senate", *Studies*, March, 1936.
[44] O'Rahilly, A.: "The Constitution and the Senate", *Studies*, March, 1936. Also see Note 43.
[45] O'Keeffe, Canon: "The Problem of the Senate", *Studies*, 1937: *Report of the Oireachtas Commission on the Second House of the Oireachtas*, 1936: Vocational provisions in 1922 and 1937 *Constitutions*: *Senate Debates* 21:299 *et seq.* 13th July, 1938.
[46] Moss, W.: *Political Parties in the Irish Free State* (1933), p. 50 and Kohn, *op. cit.* pp. 117-200.
[47] Mr. Frank MacDermot—*Dáil Debates* 67:1427, 11th May, 1937.
[48] *Ibid.*

to shorten its suspensory period—a measure of a more moderate character than that eventually resorted to—and proposed instead a Joint Committee to discuss its own re-constitution, the proposal lay on the Dáil's order paper for two years undiscussed.[49] A similar proposal made in 1936 was ignored. Given the change-resistant triennial electoral system and the absence of any charisma deriving from popular elective authority coupled with the Government's semi-revolutionary programme, it became impossible for the two Houses to work in harmony; one had to give way, and, inevitably, the Senate had to yield. Its chances of being a strong House vanished in 1928 with the referendum power and popular election; the extension of the period of complete constitutional flexibility from eight to sixteen years weakened the House further, with the result that it possessed more power than it could defend and keep. It could cripple a legislative programme, but only at its peril.

---

[49] McCracken, *op. cit.* p. 143.

Chapter Two

THE FORMATION OF
THE SENATE

1. RECONSTRUCTION

Mr de Valera's attitude toward bicameralism was never enthusiastic. The main reason for introducing a scheme for a Second Chamber into the Draft Constitution was a desire to make some concession towards groups which felt that a Second Chamber was desirable.[1] The considerable support bicameralism had in ecclesiastical, academic, commercial and opposition circles was acknowledged, and an attempt made to satisfy it. Subsequent to the coming into operation of the new constitution, Mr de Valera explained the composition and purpose of the new Chamber at length at a meeting of the Dublin Chamber of Commerce.[2]

He regarded the traditional role of the Second Chamber as guardian of the Constitution and defender of the *status quo* against Government action as being both unnecessary and rather distasteful, given the principles of democratic government.[3] He felt that the House's real value lay in its function of checking, redrafting and amending legislation.[4] At the same time, he preferred vocationalism as a basis for its composition to Norton's suggestion which would have made the Senate little more than an omnicompetent Dáil Committee, because it offered a hope of giving the House a composition distinct from that of the Dáil.[5] Vocationalism, he considered, should be used, not as a representative principle, but as a method of providing expertise, specialist information and an extra-political, if not non-political, point of view in the Oireachtas.[6] He was determined to ensure that the Senate would have a subordinate position in the Oireachtas, and would not be capable of resisting

---

[1] *Dáil Debates* 67:56, 11th May, 1937.
[2] *Irish Press*, 29th January, 1938.
[3] *Dáil Debates* 67:55, 11th May, 1937.
[4] *Dáil Debates* 69:1626, 2nd December, 1937.
[5] *Dáil Debates* 69:2082, 9th December, 1937.
[6] *Dáil Debates* 69:1420, 1425, 1426, 1st December, 1937.

the Government, particularly in foreign affairs.[7] He admitted
to a certain "hankering" for a Second Chamber himself, but he
desired an essentially revisionary Chamber, while doubting the
possibilities of complete success.[8]

The new Constitution left ample room for statutory vocational
organisation both within and outside the Oireachtas, and the
vocational formula was uncontroversial in principle. Its very
uncontroversial character made it attractive as a basis for a
new Senate.[9]

Before the decision in favour of a bicameral Oireachtas was
taken, the findings of the Commission on the Second House of
the Oireachtas were considered by the Government.[10]

The members of the Commission found it difficult to agree on
a single scheme. There were three reports, a main one signed
by the Chairman and two minority reports. The main report
was itself an amalgam agreed on by close and by no means
unanimous votes, and several reservations were recorded. A
minority report, setting out a fully-fledged alternative scheme,
was signed by eight of the twenty-three members. The signatories of the minority report were not Government supporters:
in fact, the Fianna Fáil members, in general, supported the
scheme propounded by the main report, which was to be rejected
in favour of the minority report.[11]

The Norwegian scheme of selecting the Second House from
the First House, eliminating any possibility of widely differing
composition, was considered to deny one of the main *raisons
d'être* of a Second Chamber. The idea of electing the House
from constituencies based on the traditional four provinces was
considered archaic and irrelevant in the context of a unitary
State, although the Chairman put forward such a scheme.
Joint Dáil-Senate election of the House was also mooted. It was
still argued, particularly by the Chairman, who was Chief
Justice of the State, that vocational representation was as
impracticable in 1936 as it had been in 1922 and 1928, and that
a genuinely vocational scheme would have to await the natural
development of the necessary organisational structure in Irish

---

[7] Quote from *Dáil Debates* 69:1607-21, 2nd December, 1937. Also see *Dáil
Debates* 69:2087, 9th December, 1937.
[8] *Dáil Debates* 67:59, 11th May, 1967 and *Dáil Debates* 69:2086, 9th
December, 1937.
[9] *Bunreacht na h-Eireann*: the Irish Constitution: Articles 18 and 19. Also
see *Dáil Debates* 69:290.
[10] *Report of the Commission on the Second House of the Oireachtas*, 1st
October, 1936.
[11] See *Dáil Debates* 69:1418, 1st December, 1937.

society. Nonetheless, the minority report proposed a scheme which attempted to acknowledge and reconcile the vocational principle and political realities.

This minority report concluded that revising legislation was not in itself sufficient justification for setting up a new Senate, that the primary function of such a House was to safeguard citizens' rights and democratic institutions and to prevent encroachments on them by the Executive, and that it should therefore have a direct link with the people by being able to call a referendum on non-financial legislation at least. It added that, failing this power of referendum, the House should have a limited delaying power of ninety days, so that it would never be able to hinder Government legislation seriously. Presumably it was hoped that limited powers would give the House a certain independence of political organisations and would enable it to acquire the detachment necessary to make it a competent revisionary chamber, if it were fated to become nothing more.

The signatories recommended a House of fifty, ten to be nominated by the Premier so as to hold any political balance there might be in the Chamber, and the remaining forty to be elected to four panels representing Labour, Farming and Fisheries, Education and National Development. Regret was expressed that the categories could hardly be called vocational because Labour was represented separately and not within the other panels along with ownership and management. This inconsistency, it was explained, was due to the incomplete character of vocational organisation in Ireland, and it was probably due to the fact that organised Labour was probably the only truly vocationally organised group of substantial proportions in the country.

It was suggested that candidates for these panels be nominated by vocational bodies, universities and by government ministers. The members of the Dáil would be the electorate which would choose forty senators from the panel of candidates thus formed. It was recommended that only the general outline of the scheme be entrenched in the constitution, and that the details be left to ordinary legislation.

The scheme actually adopted bore a close resemblance to the minority report's suggestion. The Constitution provides for a Senate of sixty, of whom eleven are nominees and forty-nine are elected members.[12] The nominated members are chosen by

---

[12] *Bunreacht na h-Eireann*, Article 18:1.

the Taoiseach (Prime Minister) when the election of the other forty-nine has been completed.

The two Universities in the State each elect three senators, the electorates being their graduate bodies.[13] All elections are by proportional representation.[14]

The remaining forty-three senators are to be elected from panels of candidates containing persons having "knowledge and practical experience" of

i. National Language and Culture, Literature, Art, Education and such professional interests as may be defined by law for the purpose of this panel ;
ii. Agriculture and allied interests, and fisheries ;
iii. Labour, whether organised or unorganised ;
iv. Industry and Commerce, including banking, finance, accountancy, engineering and architecture ;
v. Public Administration and social services, including voluntary social activities.[15]

From each of these panels, the Constitution stipulates, not more than eleven nor less than five senators are to be elected. There is an extra panel which does not correspond to any of those listed in the minority report, which assumed that Public Administration would be accounted for by the Taoiseach's nominees, or would be represented in the other panels. The separate Labour panel perpetuated the admitted anomaly in the report's scheme. The very general character of the categories listed in the Constitution reflects not only the complexity of the problems but also the fact that the arrangements for electing panel senators were envisaged as being provisional.

Senate elections are co-ordinated with Dáil elections, and the whole House is renewed at one time. Casual vacancies among the nominees may be filled by similar nominations while vacancies among the elected members may be filled in any way prescribed by law. Another article makes provision for the possible direct election of senators by vocational bodies in substitution for members elected through the corresponding panels. This article seems to have been intended to offset the provisional yet limiting character of Article 18 by leaving room for a long-term resolution of what was already seen as likely to be an intractable problem : the problem of determining the panel electorate, which the Constitution leaves to be determied by law.

---

[13] *Ibid*, Article 18 : 3 and 4 (i) and (ii).
[14] *Ibid* Article 18 : 5.
[15] *Ibid* Article 18 : 7 : 10.

After an initial transitional period, the Constitution could be altered only by popular referendum, thus protecting the Articles governing the Senate's composition and powers from easy alteration or removal. Articles 18 and 19, together with the Electoral Acts subsequently passed under them, define the composition of, and mode of election to, the Second House of the Oireachtas. The powers of the House are governed by Articles 20 to 24. Seanad Eireann has the power to insert amendments to non-Money Bills and the Dáil is obliged to consider them. It has the power to initiate legislation and the right to examine all Bills. However, the House must return Money Bills after twenty-one days; it may make recommendations. The House can delay ordinary Bills for ninety days. This period can be abridged by the Taoiseach if he certifies that the Bill is "urgent and immediately necessary for the preservation of the public peace and security, whether domestic or international". Such a Bill may not have the force of law for longer than ninety days unless, during this time, both Houses agree to extend the period. Two senators may become cabinet ministers.

The law, then, is given considerable scope to prescribe much of the design and construction of the House. It may define, within fairly broad constitutional limitations, the size of each panel, the mode of election to the panels, the procedure for nomination and candidature, qualifications for nominators and candidates, the method of registration of nominators and electors and the various mechanical details involved in these. It may also define the electorate and the method of election to casual vacancies. The law also names the final appellate authority in matters of nomination, registration and election.

Once the Constitution was drafted, debated[16] and accepted by the electorate, the onus was on the legislators of the Dáil and their advisers to design a workable scheme for the panel elections.

The Seanad Electoral (Panel Members) Bill, 1937, proposed originally that the electorate be the Dáil deputies who had just been elected together with all defeated candidates for the same Dáil election who had obtained at least one thousand first preference votes. This proposal was the main casualty suffered during its passage through the Dáil, and the Act differed greatly from the Bill as introduced. Disagreement concerning the pro-

---

16 *Dáil Debates* 67:45 *et seq*, 11th May, 1937.

posals was great, both within and outside the Government party :
Mr Lemass was even more determined than was his leader to
preserve the Executive's sovereignty from senatorial encroach-
ment, and urged strong Government control over the House's
personnel.[17] Again, he stated that vocationalism would not be
feasible in the Senate in the foreseeable future, because of the
fragmentary character of "functional" organisation in Irish
society.[18] He expressed his distrust of both Government and
Opposition suggestions to a special committee set up to redesign
the Bill and take some of the work out of the Dáil's hands.[19].

The Labour Party distrusted the project equally as much.
Johnson protested, at meetings of the 1936 Commission on the
Second House, that the system propounded was pseudo-
vocational, and reactionary in that ownership was represented
as well as management. Norton had no particular attachment to
the vocational concept, and both Labour leaders had condemned
the old Senate.[20] Furthermore, the Party had supported its
abolition. Norton wanted a unicameral Parliament and, if the
Government were bent on restoring the Senate, then the more
closely it was dependent on the Dáil, the better a Second House
he felt it would be.[21] When the Government abandoned the
scheme of using Dáil candidates as the electorate and propounded instead a new scheme for independent, country-wide
election to the House by the local authorities together with the
Dáil, he grew uneasy about the whole scheme, partly because of
the rather uncertain status of some of the local councils. Towards
the close of the long debate on the Bill, he warned against the
danger of the new House becoming a preserve of politicians[22],
and expressed fears that the eleven nominees would contain
unsuccessful Dáil candidates among their number.[23] He preferred the idea of a frankly political Chamber to the crypto-
political one that he felt would result from the revised Electoral
Bill.

---

[17] *Dáil Debates* 69 : 1505, 2nd December, 1937.

[18] *Report and Proceedings of the Special Committee on the Seanad Electoral
(Panel Members) Bill*, 1937, p.xxi.

[19] *Dáil Debates* 69 : 1515—Professor O'Sullivan quotes Mr Lemass, 2nd
December, 1937.

[20] See *Dáil Debates* 51 : 1876, 7th December, 1937.

[21] *Dáil Debates* 69 : 312-313 and 1408, 7th October and 1st December, 1937.

[22] *Dáil Debates* 69 : 1411-1412, 1st December, 1937.

[23] *Dáil Debates* 69 : 320, 7th October, 1937.

Fine Gael advocated both bicameralism and vocationalism, but its members differed somewhat in their belief in the feasibility of a vocational Senate. Professor O'Sullivan (Fine Gael) considered the Dáil as vocational as the Senate would be under the proposed scheme, and suggested that terms of office for senators should be different from those of deputies so as to produce a "hangover" like that produced by the triennial system and thus make the Senate distinct in composition from the Dáil.[24] Mr McGilligan (Fine Gael) felt that the system was too complicated to work satisfactorily[25], and, during the meetings of the Dáil Special Committee, he tabled an alternative scheme,[26] suggesting an electoral college of "outsiders" from all walks of life to elect a transitional House. His proposal for a permanent system was to provide a set of registers : persons and organisations on these registers would have the right to elect senators directly. For example, Fáinne-wearers who had passed the examination in spoken Irish would have the right to elect a senator directly to the Cultural and Educational Panel, as would school-teachers. For the Labour panel he suggested a register of voters consisting of the names of contributors to the National Health Insurance Fund. The Agricultural panel electorate would consist of all those who possessed a rural rateable valuation, and the Dáil would elect the Administrative panel. Mr McGilligan later altered his suggestion for the Labour panel to read "the delegates accredited to the latest Trades Union Congress". His plan, however was condemned by both the Government and Labour parties.

The legislation was both complex and controversial. It had an extraordinary career in the Legislature, being amended almost out of recognition, being referred to a Special Committee when the Government had second thoughts, after which it underwent further amendation. The Ceann Comhairle expressed his hope that the Bill should prove procedurally unique[27] — it took from 21st July to 17th December 1937 to get it through all its Stages in the Dáil: it is, perhaps, fortunate that there was no

---

24 *Dáil Debates* 69 : 304-306, 7th October, 1937. A similar point of view was expressed as late as 1958: Ralph Sutton: "A Real Seanad", *Studies*, Summer 1958.

25 *Dáil Debates* 69 : 327, 7th October, 1937.

26 See Note (18) for this and following.

27 *Dáil Debates* 69 : 2600, 16th December, 1937.

Senate at the time. The Government electoral scheme, as finally evolved after much Committee work, was enshrined in the Act.[28]

2. THE 1937 ELECTORAL ACT

Accordingly, five panels of candidates for the forty-three seats were provided for by the Seanad Electoral (Panel Members) Act, 1937. These panels were to be filled by nominations by Dáil deputies and by registered nominating organisations. Two deputies could make one nomination to any panel. To have the right of nomination, the organisations had to be registered with the Seanad Returning Officer, who adjudicated on their claims to be of vocational character, decided whether or not to accept their applications, and allocated them among the five categories of the panels. He had very wide discretion, although certain bodies, such as local authorities, similar organisations and affiliated branches of nominating bodies already registered were disqualified automatically, but he could also disqualify any body which he considered duplicated in its representation interests and services already adequately represented by a previously registered organisation.[29]

Appeals from his decisions could be made to an Appeals Committee of fifteen Dáil deputies, nine of whom had to disagree with the decision before it could be reversed.

The Act also fixed the numbers of senators to be elected to each panel as follows: Cultural and Educational, five; Agricultural, eleven; Labour, eleven; Industrial and Commercial, nine; and Administrative, seven. These figures have never been changed.

The electorate for these forty-three seats was the Dáil deputies added to seven members of each county and county borough council, selected by election within each council. In the case of dissolved councils, surviving members of the last council elected could similarly make up an electoral committee from among themselves. Twenty-one of the senators, distributed around the panels, were to be finally elected from the candidates nominated by the vocational bodies, and the other twenty-two from the candidates nominated by members of the Dáil. These seats were distributed between the two categories of nominators as follows:

---

[28] *Dáil Debates* 69:1628, 2nd December, 1937.
[29] *Seanad Electoral (Panel Members) Act*, 1937, No. 43 of 1937 in *Acts of the Oireachtas* 1937, p.807. Also *Seanad Electoral Law Commission Report*, 1959 for this and following.

TABLE 1:

Panel	Number of Seats	
	Nominating Bodies' Sub-panel	Dail Deputies' Sub-panel
Cultural and Educational	4	1
Agricultural	5	6
Labour	5	6
Industrial and Commercial	4	5
Administrative	3	4
TOTALS	21	22

The Dáil nominees possessed a majority on every panel except the Cultural and Educational one.

A subsequent Act in 1940 dealt with bye-elections. Several vacancies had already occurred in the House. It provided for a committee, selected by the bodies on the panel which had been left with a vacant seat, which was to present three nominations to the Taoiseach, who would choose the new senator from among them.[30]

The panels of candidates were made up of two nominees of the Taoiseach and two of any ex-Prime Minister to the Administrative panel, sixty-nine nominees of Dáil deputies, and the rest, not to exceed seventy-five, were to be nominated by the vocational bodies. The vocational nominations to the Administrative panel were partly controlled by the two organisations representing members of local authorities.

The vocational organisations' nominations were to be regulated and kept below the prescribed number by a complicated procedure: the number of bodies was so limited that the number of vocational nominations to a panel would not exceed thirty, and no body was permitted to have more than four nominations, the number of nominations allotted to the bodies on any particular panel always being equally distributed among them. A sliding scale was provided in the Act so that a panel with fewer bodies registered for it could receive more nominations from each body up to the maximum of four per nominating body. This meant in practice that the number of bodies which could be registered for nominating purposes for each panel would not exceed fifteen.[31]

[30] *Seanad Electoral (Panel Members) (Bye-Elections) Act,* 1940.
[31] See Note (29).

Half of the panel senators then had to have stood for election as candidates of vocational organisations. These twenty-one senators represented the vocational element in the scheme, along with the six University senators, who were intended to be considered part of the Cultural and Educational Panel, thus making it the same size as the two largest panels — Agriculture and Labour — which had eleven seats each.[32] If the vocational nominations came to fewer than the figures given above for elected nominating bodies' senators, the gaps were to be filled by nomination by the Taoiseach: this happened on the Labour panel in the first Senate election of 1938, but this proviso has not had to be invoked since.

---

[32] *Dáil Debates* 69:288, 7th October, 1937.

Chapter Three

THE DEVELOPMENT OF
THE ELECTORAL SYSTEM
SINCE 1938

1. THE 1937 ELECTORAL ACT IN PRACTICE

Mr de Valera commented in 1937 on the electoral system which had been devised for the Senate's panel seats:

> I am not claiming that this is a perfect scheme—not by any means. I say it would pass the wit of man to get a completely satisfactory scheme for a Second House[1].

The 1937 Act was soon found not to be completely satisfactory, and eventually the 1937 and 1940 Acts were repealed in favour of the Seanad Electoral (Panel Members) Act, 1947, which was itself amended by a further Act in 1954. Complaints in the Opposition press centred on the poor showing vocational candidates made in the elections[2], and the passing of the 1947 Act deprived it of its more effective ammunition.

Allegations of corrupt practices followed the second Senate General Election in 1938[3]. Following on the next election in August 1943, a Labour senator moved that a judicial investigation be carried out of the electoral process, with particular reference to allegations of corruption[4]. Fianna Fáil carried out some investigations of its own[5], and statements claiming that vote-buying had occurred were made at the Fianna Fáil Ard-Fheis of that year. The party's leadership repudiated the suggestion[6]. A conviction resulted from such an allegation after the election of 1944, one of the arguments of the defence being that other prominent candidates had also been guilty of vote-

---

[1] *Dáil Debates* 69:2086-87, 9th December, 1937.
[2] *Irish Times*, 30th March, 1938 and *Irish Independent*, 12th May, 1938.
[3] For the questions, see *Dáil Debates* 73:1 and 378, 26th October and 9th November, 1938.
[4] *Senate Debates* 28:30-60, 27th October, 1943.
[5] *Ibid*, col. 60.
[6] *Irish Independent*, 12th October, 1945: Leading Article.

buying[7]. Hopes were expressed in the Government press that reform would not be long delayed.[8].

The Department of Local Government was carrying out its own enquiry into the workings of the 1937 Electoral Act by the early months of 1945, and its officials, the press reported, were finding some difficulty in solving the problem of reform while confining themselves to the framework set up by the Constitution. Suggestions were made that Article 18 be scrapped so as to allow for a fresh start[9].

The House was criticised on other grounds also. The Commission on Vocational Organisation, set up following on a motion by Senator Frank MacDermot in 1938, reported in 1943 and, in passing, stated that the vocational character of the Senate had never been permitted to survive the workings of party conflict[10], and expressed doubt that it had ever been the intention to have it become a vocational House[11]. The Seanad Returning Officer felt that the 1938 Act had been drafted too hurriedly, and stated that the Act did not oblige him to consider nominations from a vocational viewpoint[12]. The Commission's Report was publicised widely[13].

Fine Gael moved in the Dáil in October 1945 that a committee be set up to consider possibilities of reform[14]. The motion would have come up for discussion much earlier had it not been for a General Election and for the court-cases[15].

Corruption was mainly due to the fact that only seven or eight votes were required to elect a senator, the quota being normally around this figure. The ballot-paper was in the elector's hands for two weeks so that he could fill it in at his leisure — in the presence of a vote-buyer, if required[16]. The ballot-paper was so large that it was feasible to sell a first preference vote and later convert it into a tenth preference, so

---

[7] *Irish Independent*, 22nd November and 5th December, 1944.
[8] *Irish Press*, 17th August, 1944 : Leading Article.
[9] *Irish Independent*, 13th October, 1945.
[10] *Commission on Vocational Organisation Report*: 1943, paragraphs 309, 310 and 436.
[11] *Ibid*, paragraph 5.
[12] *Commission on Vocational Organisation—Minutes of Evidence* : Evidence of Mr Wilfred Brown, p. 218. See pp. 218 and 236.
[13] *Commission on Vocational Organisation* : *Report*: 1943 for following comment on Senate. The Report was prominently featured in the *Irish Independent* 18th-21st August 1944, perhaps because its direct relevance to the Senate controversy was only seen then.
[14] *Dáil Debates* 98 : 123, 10th October 1945.
[15] *Ibid*, 124
[16] *Ibid*, 133

as to sell the first preference vote again — if anyone so trusting could be found after the first two Senate elections of 1938. Figures of between £20 and £60 were mentioned as prices for votes during a court case in 1944[17].

The ballot papers for the first election in 1938 were nearly three feet long, and made out of a sturdy, stiff paper. In 1944, there were 125 names printed on them[18].

Rumours of corruption, indignant denials by some local councillors[19] and the legal actions had convinced Mr de Valera that "there was so much smoke there was bound to be some fire under it"[20], and the Government had recognised the need for reform before the Opposition motion came to be debated.

Another defect in the system was pointed out by the Taoiseach: seven local council votes added to the votes of local deputies could, in many cases, elect a senator and thus frustrate the whole purpose of the system, which was to present an alternative to the principle of geographical representation. Any reform would, then, have to take into account the size of quotas and any possible geographical groupings of votes. Local ties could also disrupt the plans of party organisations, although the system in operation lent itself to the practice of local party headquarters' filling up its members' ballot-papers. Neither the vocationalists nor the parties were happy with the way the system had worked out. In the debate, a system involving household franchise and Northern representation was canvassed by Mr Dillon.[21]

Labour were unhappy with the Senate, and were still unimpressed by arguments in favour of bicameralism. Fine Gael and the Farmers' representatives urged increased vocationalism, Mr McGilligan suggesting a variant on the direct vocational scheme which he had put forward first in 1937. It was agreed finally to set up a joint committee of Dáil and Senate to attempt the drafting of a scheme of reform within the framework laid down in the Constitution. Despite opposition appeals in the

---

17 *Dáil Debates* 98:292, 11th October, 1945 for selling and re-selling possibilities. Several Senators and officials have confirmed the information I give here. For vote prices, *Irish Independent*, 22nd November, 1944.

18 *Irish Times*, 29th March, 1938. *Dáil Debates* 98:292.

19 For example, protest by Wicklow County Council: *Irish Times*, 13th August, 1943.

20 *Dáil Debates* 98:278, 11th October, 1945.

21 *Dáil Debates* 98:278-9 and 291, 10th and 11th October, 1945.

Senate for equal representation of senators and deputies on the committee, its membership was, in fact, weighted heavily in favour of the Dáil. The Committee reported in May 1947[22]; constitutional amendment was outside its terms of reference[23].

2. NEW REFORMS : THE 1947 AND 1954 ELECTORAL ACTS

Within the limitations of its terms of reference, the Committee made radical alterations, all of which were accepted and given substance in the Seanad Electoral (Panel Members) Act, 1947, which was passed through both Houses quickly and became law just in time to govern the Senate General Election of 1948.[24]

This Act provided for a separate election and ballot-paper for each panel and for nomination committees drawn from the appropriate nominating bodies to reduce nominations to a manageable number by ballot among their members, thus making the vocational nomination procedure indirect, in contrast to the previous system of direct nomination. These committees were also to fill casual vacancies by direct election, and replaced the restrictions laid down in the 1937 Act on the number of bodies that could be registered for a panel and on the number of vocational nominees per panel.

The qualifications required of nominating bodies were tightened up considerably: a body's objectives and activities had to relate primarily to the appropriate interests and activities stipulated by the Constitution and its members had to be representative of persons who had "knowledge and practical experience" of such activities and interests. Profit-making bodies were ineligible, as were civil servants' or local authorities' employees' associations except for those associations registered *ex officio* for the Administrative panel. Affiliates and subsidiaries of previously registered bodies were denied registration, and the organisations were required to fulfil certain requirements concerning audit, procedure and income, these last provisions not applying to "scientific or cultural bodies of national importance" if the Returning Officer saw fit.

The Appeals Committee was changed to consist of the Chairmen and vice-Chairmen of each House, and of a Judge of the

---

[22] *Joint Committee on Seanad Panel Elections*: *Proceedings and Report*. 13th May, 1947.
[23] *Dáil Debates* 108 : 2164/5, 20th November, 1947.
[24] *Dáil Debates* 108 : 2146 *et seq.* 20th November, 1947; *Dáil Debates* 109 : 342 and 380: *Senate Debates* 34 : 1587 *et seq.*

Supreme Court or High Court, nominated by the Chief Justice, to serve as Chairman with a casting vote.

The electorate was changed dramatically: senators were enfranchised as well as deputies, and they also received the right to nominate candidates to the Oireachtas sub-panels—the former Dáil sub-panels. All members of the county and county borough councils received votes. The electorate was thus nearly tripled, being increased from over three hundred to somewhat less than a thousand. Any four members of the Oireachtas could nominate to any panel, and the numbers of seats allotted to nominating bodies and Oireachtas nominees were changed from fixed numbers to minimum numbers, thus entailing a number of "floating seats" on each panel to which candidates nominated by either Oireachtas members or by nominating bodies could be elected. The effects of this change are discussed below, but the reason for it, it was explained by Mr MacEntee, was that the fixed sub-panel system could result in candidates being elected without reaching the quota, or without having received any votes. The new system, however, was not able to eliminate completely the anomalies in the election counts which resulted from the electorate preference for Oireachtas nominees.

The Clerk of the Senate became Returning Officer, a transitory provision permitting Mr Wilfred Brown to handle the 1948 election: he had been Returning Officer since 1938.[25]

Minor troubles led Fianna Fáil to re-investigate the situation when the party returned to power in 1951: an interdepartmental committee of the civil service reported on the electoral system, a Bill was introduced in the Senate, being examined by a Select Committee of that House in 1952. The Bill was enacted in January 1954.

The major change this Seanad Electoral (Panel Members) Act, 1954 made was to amend the 1947 Act by abolishing the nominating committees. In their place, a formula limited the number of nominations permitted to each body. Subject to this, every vocational nominee's name appeared on the ballot-paper, the separate panel elections being retained. The organisations registered for the appropriate panel were allowed to nominate

---

[25] Quote of Mr MacEntee from *Dáil Debates* 108:2153, 20th November 1947, *Seanad Electoral (Panel Members) Act*, 1947: no. 42 of 1947, in *Acts of the Oireachtas* 1947, p. 729.

for casual vacancies, the Oireachtas being the electorate in these cases. Subject to appeal, the Returning Officer was to decide on doubtful applications for registration as a nominating body.[26] The procedures have not been changed since 1954.

At present, then, under the provisions of the 1947 and 1954 Acts, the Cultural and Educational Panel's "professional interests"[27] are still defined as being "law and medicine (including surgery, dentistry, veterinary medicine and pharmaceutical chemistry".[28] The register of nominating bodies is kept by the Clerk and revised annually, his discretion in registration matters having been reduced considerably.

Fifty-one nominations are the most permissible for Oireachtas members, considerably fewer than the number possible under the 1937 Act, which came to over sixty. The maximum number is rarely availed of in practice.

The maximum permissible number of nominations to the vocational sub-panels depends on two factors, namely (a) the number of bodies registered for each panel and (b) the maximum number of vocationally nominated senators that could be elected to each panel, this maximum number being those seats on the panel not reserved for Oireachtas-nominated senators.

To find the number of nominations to be allocated to each body requires a rather complicated formula: the maximum number of vocational senators possible on the panel is ascertained, doubled and divided by the number of bodies registered for that panel. If the result is a fraction, the next highest whole number is taken.

Thus, after the revision of the register in March 1958, for example, there were forty-eight bodies on the register, and the number of permissible nominations worked out as follows[29] :—

---

[26] *Seanad Electoral (Panel Members) Act*, 1954; No. 1 of 1954, passed 22nd February, p. 3 *et seq. Acts of the Oireachtas* 1954. This Act was partly based on the findings of the *Seanad Select Committee on the Seanad Electoral (Panel Members) Bill*, 1952, reported 1st July, 1952. Also see *Dáil Debates* 144:67, Mr Sweetman, 10th February, 1954.

[27] *Bunreacht na hEireann*, Article 18:7:10.

[28] *How Seanad Eireann is Elected* (Department of Local Government, checked by Seanad Office), 1965. See also S. McG. Smyth: "Seanad Eireann", a series of articles in *Administration*, Vols. 15, 16 and 17.

[29] For explanation of nomination procedure and the table, see *Seanad Electoral Law Commission Report*, 1959.

TABLE 2:

Panel	1 Number of Nominating Bodies	2 Maximum Number of Vocational seats	3 Number of Nominations permissible by each Body to each panel	4 Total Number of Bodies' Nominations to Panel (i.e. Column 1 X Column 3)
Cultural and Educational	14	3	1	14
Agricultural	7	7	2	14
Labour	3	7	5	15
Industrial and Commercial	19	6	1	19
Administrative	5	4	2	10
Totals	48	27	Not Relevant	72

The number of permissible vocational nominations has remained unchanged, and is considerably greater than the number of Oireachtas nominations. While it is theoretically possible for twenty-seven vocational nominees to get elected, it is also possible for the maximum of twenty-seven Oireachtas nominees to be elected, leaving the vocational nominees with their minimum of sixteen seats. (See table below.)

When the nominations have been received by the Returning Officer, he divides the panels of nominees into sub-panels, according to whether they are nominated vocationally or by the Oireachtas. He rules on the qualifications of the nominees, subject to appeal.[30]

The voter has five votes, one for each panel. There are no plural qualifications permitted which might entitle him to more than five. He receives a list of candidates, stating by whom or by which organisations they were nominated. Five ballot-

[30] See Note (28).

papers are issued, and the election is conducted by post. It is laid down that the ballot-papers must be filled up in the presence of an "authorised person", who must countersign the voter's form of declaration of identity. "Authorised persons" are the Clerks and Clerks-Assistant of the Houses of the Oireachtas, County Registrars, Sheriffs, County and City Managers, County Secretaries and Superintendents of the Garda Síochána.[31] The "authorised person" seals the ballot envelope, and the Returning Officer may reject any ballot paper that seems to have been tampered with.

Despite occasional claims,[32] there has been little rumour of vote-buying since 1948.

The minimum numbers of candidates from each sub-panels who must be elected leave a number of "floating seats" to be filled, as explained earlier. These seats are distributed over the panels as follows[33] :—

TABLE 3 :

Panel	Number of seats	Minimum Number of senators required from each sub-panel	Number of "Floating Seats"
Cultural and Educational	5	2	1
Agricultural	11	4	3
Labour	11	4	3
Industrial and Commercial	9	3	3
Administrative	7	3	1
Totals	43	16	11

Each panel has a separate election count, the normal procedures of proportional representation being used. First preferences are counted first, but it happens sometimes that two candidates receive an equal number of first preferences : the small size of the electorate makes this occurrence more probable. If this happens, the other preferences of these candidates must be counted as well, making for a rather long-drawn-out procedure. When either the vocational or Oireachtas sub-panels

---

[31] *Ibid.*
[32] *Dáil Debates* 192 : 1292/3, 6th December, 1961. Also see *Dáil Debates* 193 : 651, 22nd February, 1962.
[33] *Seanad Electoral Law Commission Report*, 1959.

have received their maximum complement of elected senators, the votes of the defeated candidates for the filled sub-panel are redistributed before counting is resumed. The early filling of a sub-panel may lead to odd-looking results once the lower preferences are transferred to the other sub-panel.[34] As each panel has one or more "floating seats", candidates on one sub-panel may be, and have been, elected without reaching the quota. In fact, they may be elected while a candidate for the other sub-panel who has received more votes is defeated!

Invariably, the candidates on the Oireachtas sub-panels are more acceptable to the electorate than those on the vocational sub-panels. The system of allocating minimum numbers of seats is intended to prevent the electorate's wishes from dominating the election completely. Furthermore, some of the vocational nominations are not truly vocational. This is due to the large number of vocational nominations, which encourage competition between the organisations to put up candidates acceptable to the voters and capable of gaining party backing.[35]

In the case of casual vacancies, each body has one nomination, and nine members of the Oireachtas may make one nomination. The electorate is the Oireachtas.[36]

The university electorate is all graduates over twenty-one. Candidates may be nominated by two graduates, with the assent of eight others. By-elections follow a parallel procedure.[37]

As the electorate remains constant and the sizes of panels vary, the quotas vary considerably also. In 1961, for example, the quotas were[38] :

Cultural and Educational	138
Agriculture	69
Labour	69
Industrial and Commercial	82
Administrative	103

---

[34] See Note (28): for an example of the "bewildering results", see Dr T. J. O'Connell's Letter to the Editor, *Irish Times*, 6th August, 1951.

[35] *Irish Independent*, 19th July, 1954, p. 7, for an example of the effect of the "floating seat". *Irish Times*, 9th April, 1948, for a classic example of the electorate's preference for Oireachtas-nominated candidates.

[36] *How Seanad Eireann is Elected.*

[37] *Ibid.* Cf. for description of electoral and nominating procedures, S. McG. Smyth: "Seanad Eireann", articles in *Administration*, Vols. 15, 16 and 17.

[38] *Seanad General Election for Panel Members* 1965 (Seanad Office).

3. GETTING ELECTED TO THE SENATE

Candidates must campaign, as must candidates for the Dáil. Their "constituency" is country-wide, and many candidates travel around the country canvassing local councillors. Canvassing is also done by post.[39] There is a visible tendency in recent years for the number of panel senators resident in the Dublin area to shrink. This reflects a similar tendency in the Dáil. It is advantageous to have a "bloc" of votes in one county, and there have been attempts to trade "bloc-votes" with other candidates in similar control of local representatives in other areas, so that each benefits from first preference given to particular panels. This system has been known to work. Since the party allegiances of most councillors are known, candidates normally concentrate on those belonging to their own party or who are independent. Competition is therefore between candidates of the same party rather than with the candidates of other parties. Since there are no political issues to be argued, campaigning is fairly uneventful.[40] Occasionally, being a prominent official of a commercial organisation or of a trade union can be as effective a vote-getter as a more purely political attachment.

Non-partisan local councillors introduce a note of unpredictability into the election, although many independents have leanings toward a party.[41] In the 1957 Senate General Election, the two major parties gained more seats in the House than the numbers of declared supporters they had in the electorate would account for. The Labour Party, on the other hand, did not, it appears, benefit much from the independent vote. In 1943, both major parties claimed substantial "independent" support.[42] A floating vote exists: Fianna Fáil's share of the seats dropped significantly in 1954 as compared with 1951, although both elections had been held with the same local authority electorate (see table below).

Local elections are held irregularly, and are usually postponed when other more important elections are scheduled. With various exceptions, the bulk of the local authority elections are held within a few days, usually toward the end of June. Since

---

[39] *Irish Times*, 11th December, 1961. An Irishman's Diary.
[40] Senator Eoin Ryan: oral interview. *Senate Debates* 34:1700, 12th December, 1947; *Irish Times*, 9th March, 1948.
[41] *Senate Debates*, 59:358, April, 1965.
[42] Local Election Figures in *Irish Press* and *Irish Independent*, June-July, 1955, also see *Irish Independent*, July 6th, 1943.

1945, elections have been held more or less at five-year intervals, although the elections due in 1965 took place in 1967 because of the General and Presidential Elections which took place in 1965 and 1966.

TABLE 4 :

Year in which bulk of local elections took place	Senate elections affected by electorate thus formed	
1934	1938 (2 elections)	
1942	1943, 1944	
1945	1948	
1950	1951, 1954	
1955	1957	
1960	1961, 1965	([43])
1967	1969	

Due mainly to Fianna Fáil grass-roots and local government links, by 1938 the party could claim a dominance in the local authorities. In the first panel election, well over fifty per cent of the seats went to Fianna Fáil.[44] This was partly due to Labour's boycott of the election, in protest against the registration of a "mushroom" organisation as a nominating body to the Labour panel on equal terms with the TUC. The net effect of this was to award the Government three seats. Normally, Fianna Fáil wins about one-half of the panel seats and Fine Gael about thirty per cent of them. Labour usually has six or seven panel senators. Seats occasionally go to vocational, independent or minor party candidates.

The main problem for party leaders is to know how many candidates should be nominated so as to use the vote to the best advantage. The fact that prominent party men sometimes get vocational nominations complicates the situation.

In 1965, twenty-five Fianna Fáil candidates were nominated by the Oireachtas. Fourteen were elected, and those on the Labour panel were all elected. Fine Gael nominated fourteen through the Oireachtas, and nine were elected. Labour's figures were seven and four. Fianna Fáil had the allegiance of ten

[43] Department of Local Government. Also see *Senate Debates* 59 : 346 *et seq.* April, 1965.
[44] *Irish Times*, 30th March, 1958.

vocationally nominated senators, some of whom defeated Oireachtas candidates.[45]

The table below shows party strengths in the forty-three panel seats since 1938[46]. The heading "Labour" includes National Labour.

TABLE 5:

Year	1938	1938	1943	1944	1948	1951	1954	1957	1961	1965
	(1)	(2)								
Fianna Fáil	25	21	21	22	17	23	19	20	23	24
Fine Gael	14	14	13	14	14	12	12	16	11	13
Labour	1	5	7	5	7	5	7	5	7	6
Others	3	—	2	2	5	3	5	2	2	1
Uncertain	—	3	—	—	—	—	—	—	—	—

Minor parties' representatives have disappeared since 1957. The independents who occasionally win panel seats usually do so on the large panels for Agriculture and Labour where the quota is smaller.[47]

Party control over voting is by no means complete, as "surprise" votes have shown over the years. Parties sponsor two types of candidate, those whom they will recommend to the electorate and those for whom they will canvass actively.[48] Strategic scattering of nominations over the panels can help a party's campaign, and all parties try to do this.

There is a strong incentive for a party man to get a vocational nomination if he can, competition being easier.[49] Non-political candidates do not do well,[50] and vocational candidates rarely fill more than the statutorily prescribed minimum of seats. Between 1947 and 1958, this happened in only three instances

[45] Private sources. See for 1965 elections and nominations, *Irish Times*, April 14th, 23rd, 24th, 28th, May 1st and June 9th, 10th and 11th, 1965.
[46] 1938 (1), *Irish Times*, 30th March, 1938; 1938 (2), *Thom's* 1939 and oral sources; 1943, *Irish Times*, 27th August, 1943, *Irish Independent*, same date; 1944, *Irish Times*, 2nd August, 1944; 1948, *Irish Times*, 10th April; 1948, 1954, *Irish Times*, 20th July, 1954, 1951, 1957 and 1961: the figures were checked and augmented by reference to information acquired orally, wherever possible. *Flynn's Parliamentary Companion* was used also for the elections up to 1944.
[47] Examples: P. Crowley (1957); J. D. Sheridan (1957 and 1961) and S. Brosnahan (1961 and 1965).
[48] *Irish Times*, 9th January, 1962: Leading Article.
[49] *Senate Debates* 52:657-8, Senator Donegan, 17th February, 1960.
[50] Examples reported in *Irish Times*, 2nd August, 1944, 11th October, 1945, 9th April, 1948 and 11th May, 1957.

out of a possible twenty, the excess in each case being one senator. With one exception, the Oireachtas sub-panels were over-filled.[51] Despite claims that the present system represents an intensification of vocationalism in comparison with the pre-1947 system,[52] in practice it is nothing of the sort: under the old system, twenty-one senators had to have vocational nominations. Under the new system, the usual number of such nominees elected is sixteen or seventeen.[53] Senators nominated vocationally usually behave like politically nominated senators on the floor of the House, and well-known political figures have been known to defeat people prominent in the relevant vocations on the vocational sub-panels.[54]

In 1957, for example, fourteen vocationally nominated candidates and six Oireachtas candidates contested the Cultural and Educational panel, which has five seats. The minimum number of seats reserved for each type of nominee is two, and one seat is "floating". Oireachtas candidates won three of the five seats, and the two vocational seats were filled by supporters of the two major parties—one of them an ex-deputy. In the same election, on the Industrial and Commercial panel (nine seats, three "floating") three vocational candidates out of thirteen were elected, and six out of nine Oireachtas candidates were elected. The three successful vocational candidates were all prominent supporters of political parties. In the election, vocationally nominated candidates were usually the last declared elected, often without reaching the quota.[55] Over the years, many senators have had past careers as local councillors or as deputies, usually with strong party affiliations.

Mr J. D. Sheridan presents one of the few examples of an unaffiliated vocational candidate successfully running the gauntlet of the electorate. During the crucial votes on the "P.R. Bill" in 1959, he abstained, although other similarly nominated senators denied that they had any obligation to be non-partisan.[56] Since 1961, Senator S. Brosnahan has represented the INTO in the Senate while being unaffiliated politically.[57]

These are exceptional cases. Prominent senators have, over

[51] *Seanad Electoral Law Commission Report*, 1959.
[52] See for example *Senate Debates* 52:2059, 13th July, 1960.
[53] See *A Real Seanad*, Ralph Sutton: *Studies*, Summer, 1958.
[54] *Irish Times*, 9th April, 1948.
[55] *Irish Times*, 11th May, 1957. Also see note (53).
[56] *Senate Debates* 50:849 and 867, 19th February, 1959.
[57] *Senate Debates* 57:1272.

the years, denied the existence of a substantial cross-bench element in the House.[58, 59]

The university senators are usually independent, or, if politically affiliated, have an independence which arises from their mode of election, which is not controllable by party organisations. Graduates tend to vote in groups, such as secondary teachers, Cork graduates, doctors and, in Trinity, there seems to be a split by age.[60]

The "Taoiseach's eleven" are normally reliable party members. The panel and university seats are usually so evenly divided between the parties as to urge a selection of such people on the Taoiseach.

The Inter-Party Government's nominees were in as near proportion as possible to the various party strengths in the coalitions.[61] In the 1940s, Fianna Fáil nominees included veteran party workers, representatives of the Gaelic revival and of the ex-Unionists. The pattern has not changed significantly. Fianna Fáil's nominees have tended to be renominated. Since 1957, there have been more ex-deputies among them. Miss Margaret Pearse and Mrs Nora Connolly O'Brien have been nominated each time, as close relatives of the two most prominent leaders in the Easter Rising. Mr W. A. W. Sheldon has been a nominee since 1961. He had previously held a Dáil seat in Donegal as an Independent, and lost it because of the redrafting of constituency boundaries.[62] Nominees rarely "rebel", even when they do not belong to the Government party.[63]

With eleven seats at its disposal, it is virtually inconceivable that a Government could succeed in getting office and fail to gain control of the Senate.

The rural bias of the Senate electorate would make it difficult for a Party which depended for its support on the urbanised areas of the country to gain control over the House. Its electorate is also a strong encouragement for any rapidly growing party to attempt to expand its grip on local government councils: to win Senate seats a party needs a well-developed organisational structure in the local authorities and, if possible,

[58] *Senate Debates* 24:2009, 3rd July, 1940.
[59] *Senate Debates* 52:634:5, January, 1960.
[60] For campaigning and canvassing by University Graduates, I used oral sources and personal observations at 1965 Election. On Trinity Election 1961, *Irish Times*, 14th December, 1961—An Irishman's Diary.
[61] Thom's Directory, 1949, See note (9). *Irish Times*, 20th July, 1954.
[62] *Irish Times*, 30th January, 1962.
[63] *Senate Debates* 50:249 et seq., 4th February, 1959.

in the vocational bodies. The system militates against "mushroom" or revolutionary parties. In 1948, Clann na Poblachta's dramatic rise resulted in a dozen Dáil seats but none on the Senate panels. Even by 1951, its penetration of the Senate was slight.

Because of the long intervals between local elections, there is a "time-lag" between Dáil and Senate. A party which has lost popular support may be overrepresented in the Chamber. Normally, this does not matter, but it might be important in times of political stress. The 1957 Senate was elected to a great extent by the local councillors voted into office in 1955 in an election which reflected a strong swing in opinion away from Fianna Fáil.[64] The pendulum had swung back by 1957, but this was not reflected in the Senate: the House of 1957-1961 had fewer Fianna Fáil panel senators than any other House dominated by a Fianna Fáil Government.

Rather more than half the senators return to the new House after an election:

TABLE 6: *Turnover of Senators*

Senate (year)	Total Senators returning to new House	to Panels	as Nominees	to University Seats	(Dublin University)	(National University of Ireland)
1938 (2nd election)	36 (60%)	19	10	6	(3)	(3)
1943	38 (63%)	28	9	4	(3)	(1)
1944	38 (63%)	22	10	4	(2)	(2)
1948	31 (52%)	27	—	3	(2)	(1)
1951	35 (58%)	27	—	5	(3)	(2)
1954	29 (48%)	20	—	4	(2)	(2)
1957	30 (50%)	25	—	5	(2)	(3)
1961	29 (48%)	21	6	4	(2)	(2)
1965	29 (48%)	26	6	4	(2)	(2)

The qualifications required of candidates for the panels are not very stringent. Most panel senators are re-elected to the same panel, and Taoiseach's nominees are sometimes elected to the panels if the Government party loses office. Candidates have often been accepted for different panels, presumably be-

---

[64] *Irish Independent*, 7th July, 1955.

cause they have plural qualifications. "Transfers" have been made from the Administrative to the Industrial and Commercial panel and to the Cultural and Educational panel, from the Labour panel to the Industrial and Commercial panel and to the Agricultural panel. In fact, the Senate's panels ensure that the panel seats will not be occupied by forty-three practitioners of the same profession, but very little else.[65, 66] It seems, however, that insistence on qualifications is as strict as the vague provisos in the law permit.[67]

Successful candidates, then, normally have the support of a political party: one's chances of being elected on a purely vocational plank are slight. There is a tendency toward more "local men" being elected. Relatives of national figures, prominent leaders and local personalities have an advantage, as have candidates connected with local government affairs. Politicians' widows are sometimes elected. The electorate is less willing to elect "first-timers" than is the Dáil electorate, unless they have strong backing. To have a local following gives a candidate a head start. Vocational prominence is, for the most part, an incidental qualification for success.

[65] See *Irish Times*, 1st August 1951 and 27th August, 1943 and for general comment, *Irish Times*, 4th August, 1951.
[66] *Dáil Debates* 108:2164-2165, 20th November, 1947.
[67] Private oral source. Also cf. S. McG. Smyth: "Seanad Eireann" articles in *Administration*, Vols. 15, 16 and 17.

Chapter Four

THE HOUSE AT WORK —
ITS ORGANISATION
AND BUSINESS

1. PHYSICAL ARRANGEMENTS AND PROCEDURE

The Senate meets in an ornate room in the North wing of Leinster House, at the opposite end of the building from the Dáil Chamber, and on the upper storey. The division lobbies are in the southern long side of the chamber, which is oblong in shape. There is a large semi-circular alcove in the North wall, directly opposite the division lobbies.[1]

The members' seats are arranged in a semi-circle, thirty seats on each side of an aisle connecting the division lobbies and the Cathaoirleach's (Chairman's) seat, which the members' seats face. In front of the Chairman's dais there is a table for the official transcribers. On the Chairman's left there is a chair for ministers or their representatives facing the assembly, behind which there is accommodation for the minister's official advisers. On the other side of the Chair sit the Clerk and the Assistant Clerk. At the ends of the Chamber are press and visitors' galleries.

Senators speak from their places, standing. The Chair decides the order of speaking, giving favour to the front benches, which are occupied by party leaders, Government on the left, and Opposition on the right, of the Chair. There is no time-limit for speeches. The Chairman rules on relevance and has extensive power to control disorderly conduct in the House: he may adjourn the House or suspend the sitting if he considers it necessary. One motion suffices to suspend a group of senators: by contrast, in the Dáil a motion to suspend a deputy must be specially made, a new motion being required in each case. Generally, senators' standards of orderly behaviour are higher than those observed in the Dáil.

---

[1] Mac Críosta: *Leinster House* (1955), for the physical arrangements. Malone, S.: *Notes on Procedure on the Houses of the Oireachtas* (1947) for procedure.

Sittings follow those of the Dáil. The Senate normally meets on Wednesdays at 3.00 p.m., and may sit as late as it wishes. If there is a lot of business, it usually meets on a Thursday, and, perhaps, Friday. On occasion it has met on other weekdays.

Amendments must reach the Clerk two days before the discussion. Voting is by the sound of voices, but five senators may demand a formal division. The Tá (yes) lobby is on the left or government side, and the Níl (no) lobby is on the right or Opposition side, of the Chair. Twelve is a quorum, and there is no proxy voting. The Chair is not protected from party as it is in the Dáil, and changes with the Government: it is held by a Government senator, the vice-chairman normally being a member of the Opposition.

Despite proposals in 1938 that the senators sit according to their vocational panels[2], seating is by party allegiance. Labour, University and Independent senators tend to sit near the aisle, Labour just to the right of it, and the others scattered on either side, their positions not reflecting political allegiances[3].

The Leader of the House, being also the leader of the Government party or group, has the task of supervising the passage of business according to the Government's wishes. Government business is given precedence by Standing Order. Business is arranged by the Committee on Procedure and Privileges, which includes among its members the party Whips. As its composition reflects the strength of groups represented in the House, the wishes of the Leader are decisive in arranging the order in which business is to be taken.[4]

Members of the Front Benches are responsible for leading debates, but responsibilities are not allocated to them individually as they are in the cabinet and "shadow" cabinet in the Dáil.[5]

The Orders of the Day are printed before the debate and list the Bills and their stages, the motions and the adjournment in numbered order. They also list documents laid before the House, both statutory and non-statutory and include memoranda as to the times and places of the meetings of Senate and Joint Committees. Departures from the order of business usually are made if the Leader of the House considers business to be particularly urgent. Such matters are usually settled amicably with the Opposition party leaders, who have some deterrent power

---

[2] B. Chubb: *Vocational Representation in the Irish Senate.*
[3] *Senate Debates* 48: 10, 22nd May, 1957
[4] Malone, S., op. cit.
[5] See *Irish Times*, 17th June, 1966, page 6.

against any attempt to ignore their wishes, as they can do much to delay business.

Procedure in the House is similar to that in the Dáil: the existence of Government and Opposition groupings makes other similarities inevitable. Both Dáil and Senate are eccentric among "post-British" parliamentary assemblies in having the Government on the Chair's left.

2. PARTY, VOCATIONALISM, AND INDEPENDENCE IN THE SENATE

While Government-sponsored Bills normally are passed by the Senate by means of the Government's overall majority in the House, such Bills have, occasionally, been rejected, and amendments have occasionally been pressed in the face of ministerial disapproval or indifference. Such votes normally are due to 'fluke' circumstances, to "fringe" supporters of the Government defecting or absenting themselves or to neutral senators aligning themselves with the Opposition. Careless whipping has resulted occasionally in a 'snap' division defeating the Government.

The Government has only once been defeated in a division which was expected and in a capacity vote. This was the rejection in Committee of the core of the Third Amendment to the Constitution Bill, 1959, popularly dubbed the "P.R. Bill". This defeat was primarily due to the illnesses of two government senators, while the Opposition groups, the six university senators and an Independent joined forces to defeat the Bill. As previously related, another Independent senator abstained.[6] Other rejections have occurred as the result of 'snap' divisions.[7]

The House has also pressed amendments by division on the ministers. There is only one instance of the full procedure provided for conflicts between the two Houses being availed of: in 1943, amendments were made despite the Government's wishes to an Intoxicating Liquor Bill. The amendments proposed earlier closing times for public houses than those proposed in the Bill. The Dáil (and the Government) eventually had its way on the main point, but only after a Joint Conference of both Houses had been convened to resolve the conflict. It emerged during this affair that, under the Constitution, if the Senate rejected a Bill and the Dáil subsequently deemed it to have

---

[6] *Senate Debates* 50: 1301 and 1398, 11th and 12th March, 1959. The critical sections were reinserted in the Dáil and were again rejected by the Senate on Report Stage, *Senate Debates* 50: 1669 and 1672, 19th March, 1959.

[7] *Senate Debates* 57: 1392 et seq., 1st July, 1954.

assed both Houses, it could be passed only in the form in which
t left the Dáil: no amendment made in the Senate would get
hrough. Under the Constitution of the Irish Free State, the
Dáil was permitted to be more selective.[8] This position weakens
he Senate in conflicts of this type, as insistence on particular
oints may mean the loss of all the revision work done on a Bill.

In 1944 an amendment was successfully pressed on the
ninister during the discussions on the second Transport Bill of
hat year. As in the 1964 example referred to earlier, this defeat
vas caused by absenteeism due to careless whipping. Action was
aken to ensure that the amendment would not survive the final
tages of the Bill.[9]

Of sixty-three divisions in the Senate of 1938-1943, only six
ould be termed free votes: in general, the vast majority of
enate votes are on party lines. This is so despite the fact that
senator's rebellion is most unlikely to have consequences as
erious as a deputy's, which would lead one to expect that inde-
endent members would be tolerated more willingly in the
enate than in the Dáil. There are few signs that this is, in fact,
o, and developments in the last decade indicate that it may be
ecoming even less so. The vocational nomination system, the
xistence of university senators, and the fact that the Taoiseach,
ntil fairly recently, normally nominated one or two unaligned
enators all have tended to blur party allegiances somewhat, but
his does not affect the efficient working of the party system in
ne House.

The Senate of 1957-1961 was fairly evenly split between
overnment and Opposition. During the first year of its sittings
22 May, 1957—21 May, 1958), there were twelve divisions in
ne House. The pattern of voting in these twelve divisions
emonstrate well the patterns of alignment which have become
ormal and show also the extent to which party lines "blur"
or vocational or other reasons.

Four senators voted in none of these divisions, one of them
eing the Chairman, who had been nominated vocationally for
ne 1957 election. The other abstainers were a Taoiseach's
ominee, another vocational nominee and an Oireachtas nominee.
here were two divisions in which Labour opposed a combina-
on of Fianna Fáil and Fine Gael. Of the six Labour senators,
ne, a Taoiseach's nominee, opposed the Government on these

Senate Debates 27: 1697 and *Dáil Debates* 89: 843. Jan.-March 1943.
Irish Independent, 10th November, 1944.

divisions only. None of the other Labour senators supported
the Government in more than one division throughout this
period.

Excluding these two divisions, we are left with ten in which
the alignment was Fine Gael and Labour *versus* the Fianna Fái
Government. In these ten divisions, one Taoiseach's nominee, the
six university senators, eight vocational nominees and thirteen
Oireachtas senators opposed the Government more than once :
nine Taoiseach's nominees voted invariably with the Government, as did four vocational and thirteen Oireachtas senators
none of the university senators was so consistent. Two university
senators, six vocational nominees and four Oireachtas senators
invariably opposed the Government. The Fine Gael leader voted
twice for the Government, while the Labour leader invariably
opposed it. All party leaders voted in all ten divisions.

One Taoiseach's nominee, three university senators, two
vocationally nominated senators and three Oireachtas-nominated
members displayed a considerable randomness in their voting
these constituted fifteen per cent of the membership of the
House. Four of these were declared independents, four members
of the Fine Gael Opposition, and one a non-aligned Taoiseach's
nominee. Senators who vote independently are as likely to be
prominent members of the Opposition taking advantage of loose
ness of party discipline as they are to be formally independen
senators—unless, of course, a "confrontation" is in progress[10]
In order of independence, I would rate the University member
as the most uncommitted, followed by the vocationally nominated
members, the Oireachtas nominees and, lastly, the Taoiseach's
nominees. A typical Senate possesses four or five completely
uncommitted members.

Senator Hayes once commented apropos of the duties of a
senator

> I do not think there is any question of what we are asked
> to do . . . . It is not, as somebody suggested, to give advice. It is
> not getting up to say 'I think this Bill is so and so.' We are
> expected to get up and say : 'I am against this Bill, or 'I am
> for this Bill' or 'I am going to vote for the whole of this Bill
> or 'I am going to put in an amendment to Section 22'.[11]

This is, in fact, what senators normally do, and they use the
mechanics of party to do so, the leaders drawing a long and
more or less obedient "tail" behind them into the division

---

10 See *Senate Debates* 52 : 664 et seq., 17th February, 1960.
11 *Ibid.,* 667.

lobbies; in essence, there is no difference in behaviour from that observed in the Dáil.[12] The pattern of limited independence observed in the 1957-1958 period is typical: only eleven of the senators in the Senate of 1954-1957 invariably cast pro-Government votes.[13]

Formal vocationalisation has had some side-effects. In the early years of the reconstituted House, some senators seemed to believe that the Chamber was vocational or could be expected to become vocational in time. An attempt was made, in fact, to organise the Agricultural Panel senators into a discussion committee on agricultural problems. Attendances were so low that the experiment was abandoned.[14] The idea of party lines in the House has acquired a slightly disreputable tinge: during the discussions in 1948 on the selection of the domestic committees, a senator remarked that he was sure each "group" in the House would be satisfied with its representation on these committes, adding that it was embarrassing to have to refer to groups, because "we are all supposed to be independents here".[15]

3. THE BUSINESS OF THE HOUSE

Bills, whether or not they deal with the financing of Government, must be examined by both Houses of the Oireachtas before they can become law. Because of the Government's control over a majority in the House, the Senate does as much work on a Bill as the responsible Minister deems desirable: it is in the same relationship to him as the Dáil is.

Non-money Bills are sometimes sent to the Senate in a "raw" state, so that the Second Chamber in fact does most of the scrutinising, discussing and amending involved in them.

Senators vary in their contribution to legislative activity, and their records on Committee Stage give ample evidence of disparity. Some senators are aided by their parties or by the Minister. The Leader of the House proposes amendments which originally came from the Minister or, through him, from the civil service, from his party or, on Report Stage in the Senate, from advice given by senators or deputies in the form of amendments, proposed at earlier stages of the Bill. A large proportion of Government amendments are 'drafting' or verbal amend-

---

12 For figures used above, see *Senate Debates*, Vols. 48-49.
13 Ralph Sutton, op. cit., *Studies*, Summer 1958.
14 *Senate Debates* 26: 1719, 15th July, 1942, et seq.
15 *Senate Debates* 35: 25, 2nd June, 1948.

ments. Independent or Opposition amendments—especially if they show an expert knowledge of the subject—are usuall considered seriously by ministers and may result in a Govern ment amendment of the same substance at a later stage, or ma even be accepted as they stand, although usually it is felt to b preferable for the parliamentary draftsmen to reformulat them.

Much of the Senate's more individual contribution is, in fact made in this way, and can be considerable: in fact, much o the legislation which the Senate amends considerably wa 'scamped' by the Dáil because of the pressure on that House t deal with financial business and the demands made on deputie by their constituencies, parties and professions. "Conservative and "radical" amendments are frequently proposed by "con servative" and "radical" senators with little apparent regar for party wishes or views. In this, senators seem to have con siderable freedom, and a certain vocational or individualis flavour pervades much of the committee work.

For example, sixty-five amendments were tabled for th Committee Stage of the Transport (No. 2) Bill, 1944, introduce after the General Election of that year.[16] This Bill was designe to set up a national transport monopoly—Córas Iompair Eirean —to replace the railway, tramway and bus companies and t have also a partial monopoly of road haulage.

One Opposition amendment, as mentioned previously, wa accepted "accidentally". Thirty-three amendments were pro posed by the Labour leadership, most of these dealing witl employment conditions, transferability of labour, pension rights recruitment and directors' fees. Thirteen originated in Senato Gerard Sweetman (Fine Gael), and three were proposed by th representative of the Cattle Traders' Association. Amendment moved by two veterans of the Free State Senate—senator Douglas and Keane—dealt mainly with the compensation bein paid to expropriated directors and shareholders.

Mr Sweetman pointed out some drafting errors in the Bil On Report Stage, twenty-two amendments were tabled an twenty were moved. Ten were accepted, all proposed by th Government. However, of these ten, seven were substantive an had had their prototypes in amendments proposed at Committe Stage by Senators Duffy (Labour), Sweetman and Ryar

---

[16] *Senate Debates* 29: 123, 8th November, 1944 et seq.

(National University). Attention was called to the contribution made by the House, especially on points of company law.[17]

The post-war years gave the Senate a good chance to prove itself in committee work. The congestion which characterised this period was coped with (see Table on Legislative and Revisionary Work). The hurried atmosphere seems to have caused the draftsmen's work to lose somewhat in quality, because the percentage of Bills amended in the Senate sky-rocketed in 1945 and 1946. In recent years, senators' contributions to the texts finally enacted do not seem to have been quite as substantial. Even in the case of the long and involved Broadcasting Authority Bill, 1959, which was introduced in the Senate, the alterations made were not as extensive as the amount of time spent on it in committee might indicate.[18] Thirty-five amendments were tabled for committee stage on this Bill. Twenty-three were moved, and three were successful—two Government amendments, and one moved by the Fine Gael leader, which was successful only on a "tie" division and which was eliminated on Report Stage. On Report stage, two Fine Gael amendments were accepted by the Government, while seven other proposals from that party were turned down by the Minister. Neither of the successful amendments was of very far-reaching importance.

Ministers sometimes do not consider senators' amendments worth the time and trouble involved in bringing the Bill back again to the Dáil. A case in point is the Local Government Bill, 1954[19]: the Minister, apropos of amendments from both sides of the House, professed himself willing "to look into the matter". While admitting the value of the amendments, he explained that the Bill was urgent, adding

" . . . . if I have to go back (to the Dáil with the Bill), I want to go back with as few amendments as possible, or only with amendments which are essential . . . ."

No amendments were made on Report Stage either.

Senator J. C. Cole's knowledge of agricultural affairs has resulted in giving him the distinction of having had his amendments accepted as preferable to previously drafted Government amendments.[20]

---

[17] *Senate Debates* 29 : 377, 10th November, 1944.
[18] *Senate Debates* 52 : 230 et seq., 3rd February, 1960.
[19] *Senate Debates* 44 : 1139, 20th April, 1955.
[20] See *Senate Debates* 52 : 1438 et seq., 24th March, 1960, Dogs (Protection of Livestock) Bill, 1960.

Non-partisan Bills can be dealt with very effectively : a fairly typical example is afforded by the Criminal Justice Bill of 1949.[21] Twenty-eight amendments were tabled for Committee Stage, twenty-one of them Government amendments, mostly of a minor character. One had originated in a suggestion made by Senator O'Brien of National University. Senator Hearne (Fianna Fáil) moved three amendments, one of which was finally accepted on Report Stage, at which sixteen further Government amendments were passed. Some of these were in answer to points raised by Opposition or University senators in Committee, the remainder being consequential in character.

A Bill with strong political implications is often put through determinedly by the Minister with little or no amendment. Forty amendments were tabled for the Rent Restrictions Bill (No. 2) 1960. Five Government amendments were accepted, while the remainder, which came from all quarters of the Opposition, were negatived with the exception of two of the six proposed by the Fine Gael leader. Some of the six Government amendments passed on Report Stage were in response to points raised in Committee.

Government Ministers accept from the Senate whatever they consider valuable and, occasionally, they accept something unimportant for reasons of tact : they will never permit the House to force them to accept anything, unless there is massive and vocal support for it elsewhere.

In some years, over 25% of non-money Bills have had amendments attached to them there, and individual Bills have been transformed in Committee, amendments being accepted directly from both sides of the House.[23] Since 1948, there has been a gradual increase in the number of ordinary Bills amended, its fluctuations following approximately the fluctuations in the overall flow of legislation. The number of money Bills has similarly shown an increase, so that more legislation of both types is being passed by the House, while the number of Bills being amended has shown a proportionate increase.

Good committee work is the most formidable item on the

---

[21] *Senate Debates* 37 : 2 et seq. and 50 et seq., 12th October and 26th October, 1949.

[22] *Senate Debates* 52 : 1702 et seq. and 1954 et seq., 21st June and 6th July, 1960.

[23] *Senate Debates* 54 : examples, Pigs and Bacon (Amendment) Bill, 1961 and Poisons Bill, 1960 debated June 1961.

Legislative and Revisionary Work of the Senate 1938–1966
(Source: Senate Proceedings 1938–1966)

Year	Legislation					Revision			Percentage of non-Money Bills amended
	Total Bills dealt with	Total Money Bills dealt with	Total non-Money Bills dealt with	Money Bills passed with recommendation	Non-Money Bills passed with amendment	Amendments rejected by Dáil	Amended Bills accepted by Dáil with alteration	Bills rejected by Senate	
1938	28	11	17	—	2	—	—	—	12%
1939	36	8	28	—	8	—	1	—	28%
1940	35	6	29	1	6	—	1	—	20%
1941	29	6	24	—	7	—	—	—	35%
1942	27	6	21	—	9	—	1	—	40%
1943	24	6	18	—	5	—	—	—	28%
1944	22	6	16	—	6	—	—	—	28%
1945	38	6	32	—	11	—	1	—	31%
1946	37	10	28	1	13	—	2	—	45%
1947	50	13	38	—	7	—	—	—	22%
1948	24	6	18	—	—	—	—	—	—
1949	34	9	25	—	3	1	—	—	12%
1950	35	7	28	—	3	—	—	—	11%
1951	29	11	19	1	2	—	—	—	10%
1952	33	8	25	—	5	—	—	—	20%
1953	38	12	26	—	2	—	—	—	8%
1954	38	13	25	—	4	—	—	—	16%
1955	31	6	25	—	3	—	—	—	12%
1956	48	13	35	—	8	—	—	—	24%
1957	33	10	23	—	6	1	—	—	24%
1958	37	6	31	—	4	—	—	—	12%
1959	44	12	32	—	5	—	—	1	16%
1960	45	15	30	—	7	—	3	—	26%
1961	47	10	37	—	7	—	—	—	19%
1962	48	12	26	—	6	—	—	—	23%
1963	34	11	23	—	5	—	—	—	21%
1964	38	17	21	—	4	—	1	1	19%
1965	25	7	18	—	4	—	—	—	22%
1966	28	3	25	—	5	—	—	—	20%

work list of a conscientious senator—in contrast to that of a conscientious deputy.

The Dáil once rejected a Senate recommendation on a Money Bill, in 1947. Government attitudes toward Money Bills financial legislation in the Senate are particularly proprietorial. Such Bills often have a long Second Stage (i.e. General Debate) in the House, usually because of those senators whose training enables them to speak authoritatively on the economic situation, economic or financial policy or on the provisions in detail. By contrast, committee treatment is cursory.

The Senate has initiated more Government-sponsored legislation since 1947, but these Bills represent only a small fraction of the volume which comes up to it from the Dáil: typically, one or two Senate Bills are passed by the Dáil every year. Up to 1948, the Senate initiated no legislation and sixteen Bills were initiated in the Senate in the period from 1948 to March 1963.[24] Most of these were introduced on an experimental basis by the Inter-Party Governments. From 1957 to March 1963, Fianna Fáil had only one Bill initiated in the Senate—the Broadcasting Authority Bill, 1959.[25] This was done for convenience, not as a precedent for a new practice[26].

However, following upon a debate in 1963 in the course of which it was represented by several senators from various parts of the House that it would be desirable to have non-controversial or technical Bills initiated in the Senate, more Bills have been introduced in the Senate.[27]

Neither Private Bills nor Private Members' Bills bulk very large in the House's timetable. A committee deals with consolidating legislation.

Motions by individual senators are the main non-legislative business to go on the floor of the House, and often these motions have to wait for months before being allotted debating time. Motions approving or endorsing Government policy are normally carried with little or no debate.

However, motions which lead to a general debate—whether raised on the adjournment or otherwise—often have a kinship to the parliamentary question, a fact which has occasionally been resented by Ministers, as the parliamentary question does not exist in the Senate. These motions may refer to some broad

[24] *Senate Debates* 56: 474, 13th March, 1963.
[25] See *Senate Debates* 52: 597, 10th February, 1960.
[26] *Senate Debates* 56: 473-475, 13th March, 1963.
[27] *Senate Debates* 56: 409, 699 and 1687.

field of policy, ask the Minister to explain his department's policy, criticise that policy or request changes in it. When legislative business is slack, motions have more time given to them, and in many ways they constitute the House's most characteristic contribution to political affairs. During 1966, Senator Fitz-Gerald's motion on manpower policy was thoroughly debated and reported, while Dr Sheehy Skeffington's motions on aspects of the educational system have been controversial and have given occasion for national debates on educational policy.[28] Professor Quinlan has been active in this field too.

If the Government considers the motion tendentious or irrelevant, it may neglect to send a minister or other representative[30]. This has been the practice of both Fianna Fáil and Inter-Party Governments.[31] At least once, a walk-out on the part of the Government senators in protest against an aggressive Opposition motion has occurred.[32]

This incident, which occurred in 1958, was followed by a motion protesting against ministerial non-attendance.[33] At this juncture, the Opposition's morale had risen as a result of the defeat of the "P.R. Bill", and the Senate saw much more political conflict than it had for some time. The Government's reaction to a 'forward' policy on the part of the Opposition senators was quick.[34] In answer to the Fine Gael leader's query as to their attitude toward the motion in the Senate[35], the Taoiseach summarised the Government's attitude. The Senate should not, it was felt, discuss financial policy outside motions or recommendations on Money Bills, nor should it, in general, discuss foreign policy. Neither should the House debate a motion which implied formal censure of Government policy or administration unless such a question should arise in the course of examining legislation or statutory regulations. Ministers were responsible to the Dáil, not the Senate, he remarked. Finally, the Senate should not debate the conduct of Dáil elections, as this was outside its province.[36]

Motions are the essential vehicle by which the Senate can

---

[28] See Coogan, T. P., *Ireland Since the Rising*, p. 140.
[29] See, for example, his motion on post-primary education, *Senate Debates* Vols. 57-58; its final fate, 58: 1305 et seq.
[30] *Senate Debates* 51: 107, 29th April, 1959.
[31] *Senate Debates* 45: 983, 15th December, 1955 and 51: 1095 et seq.
[32] *Senate Debates* 51: 644 et seq., 29th July, 1959 and *ibid*: 545.
[33] *Senate Debates* 51: 1082 et seq., 25th November, 1959.
[34] *Senate Debates* 51: 775-6, 30th July, 1959.
[35] *Senate Debates* 51: 1087, 25th November, 1959.
[36] *Senate Debates* 51: 1109-1117, 25th November, 1959.

debate its own constitution and evaluate itself : motions in the Senate have preceded every move to reform the House's constitution, and instigated the setting up of several commissions including that on Vocational Organisation, which reported in 1943 and one on the Revival of the Irish Language, which reported in 1965.[37]

In recent years, motions have been allotted less time : some have been given odd half-hours stretching over periods of months : much of the reluctance on the part of Ministers to attend these debates stems from the fact that they can drag on indefinitely, the Minister being expected by some senators to attend each time it comes up. There are prospects that a reform of Standing Orders, putting a time-limit on motions and reserving an extra day in the week for their debate may be initiated.[38]

The decline in the number of motions is illustrated by the following examples : in 1939, nine motions were debated at length, in 1942, twelve, in 1959, three, and in 1962, two.[39] Motions appear to have become more partisan in tone in the post-war years.

The Government is particularly anxious to have its legislation dealt with quickly in the House on three principal occasions. These occasions are times of unexpected emergencies, periods before and after a General Election, and the period leading up to the Summer Recess. The last occasion is institutionalised by the nature of the relationship between the two Houses which makes the Senate keep in step with the Dáil : In 1961 the Defamation Bill was passed by the Senate in five minutes on the 9th August—just before the Oireachtas rose for the Recess —during the course of an exceptionally late sitting. Several other Bills from the Department of Justice were passed on the same occasion. On this occasion, the imminence of a General Election compounded the urgency.[40] Furthermore, a controversial and important debate on a motion had been allotted generous time during July : on 12 July the legislative flood started : the House found itself with nineteen Bills to deal with before the Summer Recess, among them the Finance and Ap-

---

[37] Motions in *Senate Debates* 21 : 300 et seq., 13th July, 1938 and *Senate Debates* 48 : 1451 et seq., 30th January, 1958.

[38] *Senate Debates* 58 : 1305 for example.

[39] *Senate Proceedings* 1939, 1942, 1959 and 1962.

[40] *Senate Debates* 54 : 1909 et seq., 9th August, 1961.

propriation Bill.[41] On the 3rd August it was announced to the House that it was proposed to take the business

" .... as on the Order Paper—Numbers 1 to 9 inclusive"[42]

Senator's reactions were varied, but mainly ironical. The Government Leader commented, aptly enough,

We have a job to do which has been presented to us by Dáil Eireann and we have to do it. The length of time it will take to do that will depend, as I have said, on the members of the House, the number who will speak, and the length of their speeches.[43]

Admittedly, 1961 was an exceptional year, but the July "bottleneck" has become a regular and increasingly serious problem, and is mainly due to the Dáil's schedule being fixed by the necessity of devoting the March-July period to the financing of Government.[44] Thus, when the Dáil adjourns in July, a large number of Bills are unloaded onto the Senate to deal with as best it can. Amendment cannot be conveniently done, as the Dáil would have to be reconvened; this has never been done.[45] Overloading of this sort occurred again in 1964 and led to sharp complaints from Opposition speakers.[46]

TABLE 8 :

The Legislative "Bottleneck".[47]

Year	1949	1950	1951	1952	1953	1954	1955	1956	1957	1958	1959	1960	1961	1962
No. of Bills signed during year	33	34	31	39	39	30	48	29	39	44	47	47	47	38
No. of Bills signed during July & August	15	8	12	6	8	4	8	13	9	13	16	12	24	13
Approximate percentage of Total	45%	24%	37%	19%	20%	10%	24%	27%	35%	31%	36%	26%	51%	54%

[41] *Senate Debates* 54 : 1070 : Order of Business, 12th July, 1961.
[42] *Senate Debates* 54 : 1603 : Order of Business, 3rd August, 1961.
[43] *Senate Debates* 54 : 1716, 4th August, 1961.
[44] See *Senate Debates* 56 : 461-2, 13th March, 1963.
[45] See *Senate Debates* 56 : 459 et seq., 13th March, 1963.
[46] *Ibid.*
[47] Source : *Senate Proceedings* 1949-1962.

General Elections have the effect of intensifying legislative activity or causing a moratorium on it—or even a combination of both, giving a "go-stop" effect. In the years 1949 and 1961 over forty percent of the legislation was enacted during the six-week periods before the long recess: in 1949, however, as the total volume of legislation was small, the "bulge" did not become a bottleneck.[48]

The problem was debated in the Senate in 1963 as part of a wider motion suggesting that the Senate be permitted to initiate more Bills, that something be done to ensure a regular flow of legislation from the Dáil and that there be an end to

. . . . the practice of presenting Bills to the Seanad at times of the year when no effective consideration can be given to them.[49]

Government speakers supported the request for more initiation in a guarded manner, but pointed out that the Government could not be expected to regulate its legislation to suit the Senate. It was pointed out by the Taoiseach that the Cabinet would not, normally, have complete control over the amount of time the Dáil spent on particular businesses. Bills were introduced in July so as to ensure that there would be work to do after the Summer recess, and if the Senate wanted to do its work conscientiously, it would have to meet in August. The 1961 situation had been exceptional, and succeeding years had been more leisurely.

Despite this debate, conflict arose in 1964, over the question of 'rushing' legislation, between Opposition leaders and the Minister for Justice.[50]

In 1965, a somewhat similar situation arose, and the "bottleneck" was complicated by the Succession Bill and expectations of a General Election: The Prices Bill was passed on the 29th July in sixty seconds flat. On the 4th August, the Leader of the House thanked the Opposition leaders for their co-operation during the "awkward situation" the Succession Bill had created. There was no repetition of the events of 1961.[51] Senator Hayes,

[48] See *Senate Debates* Vols. 36, 37 (1948-1949).
[49] For this and ensuing debate, *Senate Debates* 56: 459 et seq., 13th March, 1963.
[50] *Senate Debates* 57: 1408-09, 1st July, 1964.
[51] *Senate Debates* 59: 933, 4th August, 1965.

Fine Gael Senate leader, retired from the House in the General Election of that year. With his departure, the question of the Senate's role in the legislative process was shelved, temporarily at least.

"Rushing" legislation is not merely a recent phenomenon: in 1951, for example, Fianna Fáil returned to power and several Bills were passed in one short sitting—one of them in sixty seconds—with no opposition from a sparsely attended Senate whose members were presumably out campaigning for the impending Senate election.[52]

4. SITTINGS OF THE HOUSE

The Dáil normally meets on more than seventy days in a year —about three times as often as the Senate does—and daily sittings tend to be longer than the Senate's: the Dáil sits, on average, for nearly four times as many hours per year as does the Senate. The Second House normally finishes its business before 10 p.m., and, during the war years, it finished an hour earlier because of transport difficulties.[53] Despite the increase in the volume of business, the number of sitting days per year has not increased significantly.

Senators are, for the most part, part-time legislators and cannot give extra days of the week to legislative business, and therefore prefer to sit late than to meet again in the same week.

In general, a busy period is marked by the House's meeting twice or more than twice a week, especially if the sittings are later than usual. The early war-time period, the busy post-war period, and the more consistently active period since 1956 are reflected in the incidence of late sittings since the financial crisis of that year, but not in any noticeable increase in sittings days. The House tended to have more sittings in a week during the war years than it does at present. This may be connected with the transport situation, and also it seems probable that the professional men who sit in the House to-day are less able to spend much of the working week away from their occupations than were the businessmen of twenty years ago (see below, Chapter V). This is, of course, mainly conjecture.[54]

---

[52] *Senate Debates* 39: 1184 et seq., 11th July, 1951.
[53] *Senate Proceedings* and Malone, S., op. cit.
[54] Source for table: *Senate Proceedings* 1938-1962.

TABLE 9 :

Year	Number of times Senate met	Number of times Senate met more than once a week	Number of late sittings—i.e. after 10 p.m. (9 p.m. in war years)
1938	18	5	3
1939	31	12	5
1940	25	5	3
1941	30	9	7
1942	31	11	—
1943	27	12	—
1944	25	13	—
1945	32	13	3
1946	46	18	5
1947	37	17	7
1948	20	9	—
1949	25	10	4
1950	28	9	1
1951	21	4	—
1952	24	5	—
1953	24	6	2
1954	16	3	—
1955	23	6	—
1956	26	10	8
1957	19	5	5
1958	18	3	6
1959	28	11	6
1960	28	6	10
1961	30	10	13
1962	18	4	6

5. SENATE COMMITTEES

Like the Dáil, the Senate has a Committee on Selection to choose all other House Committees and the Senate representation on Joint Committees. The eleven members of this committee are nominated on a motion put by the House Leader. It is multi-partisan; in 1961 after the General Election of that year its membership consisted of six Fianna Fáil members, three Fine Gael, one Labour and one Independent.[55] Its purpose is, as a senator described it,

[55] *Senate Debates* 48 : 74-76, 5th June, 1957.

 . . . . to iron things out to the satisfaction of the numerous independent groups comprising the House[56]

In 1957, as in 1961, the Government had control of a majority of the members of this Committee. The Library and Restaurant Committees are Joint. The Joint Committee on Standing Orders (Private Business) has as chairman a member of the Oireachtas nominated jointly by the Speakers for both Houses: in 1961, a Fine Gael senator was chairman of this committee. Another Joint Committee handles consolidation Bills. Like the Dáil, the Senate possesses a Committee on Procedure and Privileges. In 1961, its composition was similar to that of the Committee on Selection.[58]

The Committee on Statutory Instruments is of quite a different type. Consisting of nine senators, it was set up first in 1948[59] and became quite influential and wide-ranging in its activities, having been reconstituted as a routine matter by every House elected since 1948. It was ante-dated and inspired by the Westminster Committee on Statutory Instruments (1944) and the similar 1946 Committee of the Stormont Parliament.[60] Even before 1948, such a Committee had been suggested by several senators and it had also been suggested that a Joint Committee might be preferable to the Government. However, Senator Duffy (Labour) moved its establishment, and it was accepted by all parties.[61] It is empowered to examine every Statutory Instrument made and to call the Senate's attention to any instrument which demands that payments be made by or to any organ of State, or which declares itself unchallengeable in the Courts. It can also call the House's attention to an Instrument which stretches the Statute's meaning or "whose form or purport . . . calls for elucidation".[62] It can require Instrument-making authorities to explain their statutory orders by memorandum or by representative.[63] No one party has a majority on this committee. In 1962 and 1965, three of the members of this Committee had legal training. In recent years, it has had less work to do as the more glaring irregularities in Statutory Instruments

---

[56] *Senate Debates* 35: 25, 2nd June, 1948.
[57] *Senate Debates* 48: 74-76, 5th June, 1957.
[58] *Senate Debates* 55: 52-3, 116 and 224.
[59] *Senate Debates* 35: 584, 29th July, 1948.
[60] Donaldson: *Some comparative aspects of Irish Law*, p. 189.
[61] *Senate Debates* 35: 584 et seq., 29th July, 1948.
[62] *Ibid.*
[63] *First Report of the Select Committee on Statutory Instruments*, 31st July, 1963.

have been eliminated through the Committee's influence. Much of the research and examining work is done by a secretariat drawn from the Oireachtas staff.[64]

Between January and April 1955, the Committee examined 102 documents, called attention to sixteen: two were annulled.[65] Again, between March 1962 and July, 1963, the Committee examined 233 documents, and called attention to only eleven. During this period it met eleven times, staying in session about an hour.

The Committee not only criticises Orders, but also lays down requirements concerning the form of future instruments. It also guards against delegation of legislative power which is not sanctioned by statute.[66]

There is some truth in the claim that the Committee does not have the secretariat, power or resources for deeper investigation into administrative practices.[67] Against this, it was never designed for an ombudsman-like function, but rather to deal with certain specific types of administrative irregularity defined by legal formulae. Its authority is negative and *in terrorem*: it can recommend but cannot order.

6. THE SENATORS: THEIR WORK AND REMUNERATION

Attendance rates at the Senate are better than those at the Dáil: it is rarely necessary to count a quorum—much more rarely than it is in the Lower House.[68] While attendances as reckoned by signing the roll are not true indicators of how many were present at the debates, they give an indication as to how attendances vary from time to time. During 1941, the average attendance, calculated in this manner, was forty-seven; in 1959 and 1962 the figures were forty-six and fifty respectively. Lowest attendances occur toward the end of July; the approach of the Summer Recess causes the House to empty gradually. Numbers present have varied from the middle fifties to the lower twenties, critical votes and important business usually sending up the attendances.[69]

The "silent senator" is not as common as he used to be. The Senates of 1948-1951 and 1954-1957 each possessed two members

64 Oral interviews.
65 Donaldson, op. cit., p. 189.
66 See note (63).
67 T. P. Coogan, *Ireland Since the Rising* (1966), p. 141.
68 *Senate Debates* 52: 652, 28th February, 1960: Dr Sheehy Skeffington.
69 *Senate Proceedings* 1941, 1959 and 1962.

who never spoke, while the Senates of 1951-1954 and 1957-1961 possessed, respectively, six and five such members.[70]

In the Senate of 1938-1943, fourteen members spoke, on average, at least once every time the House met; the figure for the Senate of 1948-1951 was thirteen, but the figure for 1957-1961 was twenty-one.[71]

In the three Senates mentioned, twenty-one, eleven and fourteen senators spoke five times at most annually. The bulk of these senators used to be contained in the panel seats, but the position has improved considerably. If we exclude the Taoiseach's nominees, the numbers of these "nearly silent" senators were seventeen, nine and ten. Again, if the university senators are excluded, the figures for the remaining forty-three panel senators in these three Senates are sixteen, eight and eight.[72] More senators are talking than formerly: the overall annual speaking averages of senators in those three Senates were fifteen, eighteen and twenty-three.

These changes are probably connected with the increasing demands made by the House's business, the composition of the House, and a feeling among senators and parties that the House should be a start rather than an end to a political career. The increase which occurred in recent years in the number of Dáil deputies who started their political careers with a Senate seat is indicative of the trend.

Some senators have constituency work similar to a Dáil deputy's: occasionally they complain about its volume.[73] However, as a rule, they have very little in comparison with the amount a deputy has. Nor do their seats depend on their pleasing constituents. The hardest-working senators are the party leaders[74], and senators normally resident in certain constituencies where their parties are weakly represented and who find themselves "playing the part of deputies".[75] Dublin senators are less affected by this, and the burden is more likely to fall on senators resident in rural areas.[76] The burden of work is uneven: some university senators have complained of being underworked![77] However, Senator Mullins remarked

---

[70] *Index to Senate Debates.*
[71] *Ibid.*
[72] *Ibid.*
[73] *Senate Debates* 57: 1240, 24th June, 1964.
[74] *Senate Debates* 57: 1259, Senator McGuire.
[75] *Senate Debates* 34: 294 et seq., 9th July, 1947, Senator Baxter.
[76] Senator Eoin Ryan, orally.
[77] *Senate Debates* 57: 1233 et seq., and 1263, Senators Stanford and Ross.

.... there are country senators here .... who from the time
they go home do not get ease or peace until the time they leave
again for the Seanad[78]
It has been suggested, however, that senators are, if anything,
overpaid.[79] [80] The explanation of these varying opinions is, of
course, that there is tremendous variation between the amounts
of work of a "constituency" character done by senators. Senator
Hayes commented in 1947

It should not be beyond the wit of this House to devise a
system whereby the persistent non-worker in the Seanad
could be dealt with.[81]

A sure indication of the downgrading of the Second Chamber
is given by the fact that, while senators' and deputies' allowances
have been the same previously, since 1938 senators' allowances
have been "pegged" at a lower level than deputies'.[82] Apparently
it was reckoned that, on average, a senator did two-thirds of
the work of a deputy and therefore should get a proportionate
payment.[83] In the financial year 1964-1965, deputies' travelling
expenses were four times as large as senators'. A deputy's expenses were, on average, double those of a senator. The Senate
cost about one-sixth of the total money voted for the Houses of
the Oireachtas.[84]

Unlike a deputy's, a senator's work is rarely a fulltime job.[85]
Like a deputy, however, a senator may do himself more good
by maintaining liaison with the voters than by making well-
thought out speeches, and may benefit more from party work
than from work in Committee in the House. A panel senator
may have to show himself to be active in local government, and
those senators who are less eloquent on the floor of the House
may be out cultivating their electoral gardens. A veteran senator,
it is reported, once advised a newcomer to the House never to
"open his mouth" on the floor "whatever the provocation".[86]

7. THE WORK OF THE SENATE OF THE IRISH FREE STATE

The record of its predecessor, notwithstanding the differences

78 *Ibid.*, 1245.
79 *Senate Debates* 34: 266 et seq., 9th July, 1947.
80 Examples: *Ibid.*, 378, 16th July, 1947, Senator Mrs. Concannon;
   Senate Debates 34: 294, 9th July, 1947; and
   Senate Debates 55: 1690, 19th December, 1962, Prof. Quinlan.
81 *Senate Debates* 34: 379, 10th July, 1947.
82 For history of allowance scales, see *Senate Debates* 34: 266 et seq., and
   48: 627, 10th July, 1957.
83 *Senate Debates* 57: 1224, 24th June, 1964.
84 *Estimates for Public Services* for year ending 31st March, 1966.
85 *Senate Debates* 55: 1690, 19th December, 1962.
86 *Irish Times*, May 9th, 1957: An Irishman's Diary.

in the political situation, affords a perspective on the activities of the present Senate. It seems undeniable that the Free State Senate left a deeper imprint on legislation. It dealt with a greater number of Bills annually, and amended more of them.[87] This was due primarily to the fact that it was better able to enforce its views and also to the fact that the Government had less control over its activities, even during the Cosgrave era. The inexperience of both the Cumann na nGaedheal and Fianna Fáil governments gave more scope for amendments. During the years 1923-1935, the Senate sat an average of forty days annually. The present House averaged twenty-seven days annually during the years 1939-1962, and only once exceeded its predecessor's average—in 1946.

---

[87] Figures for Irish Free State Senate are for completed years 1923-1935: Donal O'Sullivan, the *Irish Free State and its Senate*, Appendices B and H. Figures for modern House are for years 1939-1962.

Chapter Five

THE COMPOSITION
OF THE SENATE

It is not possible to discuss usefully the occupational and age classification of the personnel of the Senate as a whole because of the fact that it can be divided, according to mode of election or appointment, into at least three main groups—the Taoiseach's nominees, the senators elected for the university constituencies and the panel members, limiting that term to the remaining forty-three. This last group can itself be divided into two sub-categories: nominating bodies' nominees and Oireachtas nominees. Some breakdown of the membership into these classifications is necessary to show how the House is built up, what contribution to the total is made by each system of entry, how it compares with the Lower House and where it diverges from it.

The Tuairim research group on the Composition of the Dáil picked the four Dáils of 1944, 1948, 1961 and 1965 for their survey; the composition of the Senates of these four years has been analysed in this study and put alongside these figures for comparison. The four years selected present a fair cross-section of the Senates elected since 1938, since the first was elected under the 1937 Electoral Act, the second under the unrevised 1947 Act and the last two under the 1947 Act as amended in 1954. The 1948 Senate was dominated by the first Inter-Party Government and the other three by Fianna Fáil governments.[1]

1. *Post-Secondary School Training*
The Tuairim survey found that the most noticeable change in the Dáil's overall composition over the last twenty years has been in the educational standard of the deputies. A similar change is visible in the Senate, where the university representatives intensify further the professional flavour of the assembly. The number of professionally-trained or university educated people

---

[1] Tuairim: Pamphlet No. 15: *Dáil Deputies—Their Work, Its Difficulties, Possible Remedies*, written by John Whyte (1966).

in the Taoiseach's eleven shows little pattern in the four years examined, while the figure for the forty-three panel members went up strikingly, in fact at a much higher rate than that observed for Dáil deputies in 1961. In 1965 this figure actually declined but, by coincidence or design, Mr Lemass's nominees included sufficient such people to offset the low figure for the panels and give a high percentage to the House taken as a whole. Even if the university members are excluded, five or six more university—or professionally—trained members were elected or nominated to the House than in the 1940s. The table gives the figures for the four sample Houses, with the figures for the Dáil included for comparison.[2] The percentages refer to the categories listed.

TABLE 10 :

Year	1944		1948		1961		1965	
	Number	Percent	Number	Percent	Number	Percent	Number	Percent
Dáil	30	22	32	22	40	28	43	30
Senate:								
Panels	8	19	10	23	18	40	13	30
Universities	6	100	6	100	6	100	6	100
Nominees	5	45	4	36	3	27	6	54
Total House	19	32	20	33	27	43	25	42

Disregarding the presence of the university senators, there is a persistently higher figure for professionals in the Senate than in the Dáil. Whatever criteria decide the choice of the electorate for the panels, post-secondary formal training does not rank high among them, as the rather random figure for 1965 seems to indicate. It is possible that Mr Lemass tried to fulfil the avowed intention that the nominating powers be used to compensate for any inadequacies in the panel representation.

[2] Table Constructed from
Tuairim figures for Dáils of 1944, 1948, 1961 and 1965. Senate figures from *Thom's Directory* 1945 and 1949 and Flynn's *Oireachtas Companion* 1945. There were very few gaps. Those there were were filled in from other biographical material and are probably accurate.
There have been no comprehensive *Thom's Directories* since 1958; Senate of 1961 from old *Thom's Directories* and evidence of the senators' occupations. Professor Chubb's parliamentary questionnaire supplied the bulk of the 1965 information.

In the House as a whole, professionalism is ten per cent more intensified than in the Dáil.

The panel system plays a part in this. The Cultural and Educational panel in each of the four Houses examined contributed five senators with these qualifications. The other thirteen elected to the panels in 1961 were scattered around the panels, five being on the Industrial and Commercial panel, four on Labour, three on Agriculture and one on Administrative. Generally, the Cultural and Educational and the Industrial and Commercial panels tend to contribute more professional people to the House. The vocationally nominated section of the members contributes a disproportionate share of such senators : in 1961, nine of the eighteen panel senators with post-secondary training were the nominees of vocational bodies, and the remaining nine constituted one-third of the Oireachtas-nominated senators. There were three vocationally nominated senators with such training on the Labour panel, two each on the Industrial and Commercial and Cultural and Educational panels and one each on the Agricultural and Administrative panels.

One-third of the Oireachtas nominees had such training, a percentage somewhat higher than that for the Dáil elected that year. The nine Oireachtas nominees included Mr Eamon Kissane, a veteran Fianna Fáil lawyer and a senator since his defeat in the Dáil election of 1948; Professor Michael Hayes, Fine Gael leader in the Senate, veteran parliamentarian and ex-deputy, and Mr Eoin Ryan, a barrister and son of the Minister for Finance. The nine "vocational" professionals included Professor James Dooge of Cork, chairman of Fine Gael; Professor Liam O Buachalla, Cathaoirleach and a member of Fianna Fáil; Mr E. A. McGuire, a veteran senator, a Fine Gael supporter and president of the Employer's Federation; and Mr Séan Brosnahan, secretary of the Irish National Teachers' Organisation and unattached politically.

The panel system does seem to ensure that professional men from both parties who, perhaps, would not be good electioneers, and others whose vote-catching capacities had been seen to have evaporated are kept in touch with Parliamentary affairs and enabled to contribute to the Oireachtas' work. Some of these were "retired" to the Senate, but many of them are anything but retired : to these, politics is a peripheral activity, their main energies and interests being directed toward their business, associations and professions so that it is a moot point as to whether their professional vocations give any real guide as to their "political" or "vocational" character as senators.

2. AGE-DISTRIBUTION

Difficulties were encountered in determining the ages of senators : many of them, like deputies, do not supply their birth-dates with other biographical information. In many of these cases, rough estimates of age were made based on other biographical information or based on the lengths of their political careers, guesses by acquaintance or other incidental information about them. A tentative classification into three groups—under forty, forty to fifty-nine, and sixty and over—has been made. The table probably reflects actuality reasonably well, and it is to be hoped that errors tend to cancel one another out. The percentages in the table refer to the total member-ships of the Houses : it is to be noted that the membership of the Dáil varies because of constituency revision : in 1944, there were 138 seats in the Dáil; in 1948, 147 seats, and in 1961 and 1965 there were 144 seats.[3]

TABLE 11 :

Year House	1944				1948				1961				1965			
	Senate		Dáil		Senate		Dáil		Senate		Dáil		Senate		Dáil	
Age Groups	No.	%	No.	%	No.	%	No.	%	No.	%	No.	%	No.	%	No.	%
Under 40	4	7	18	13	3	5	20	14	2	3	28	19	4	7	37	26
40 - 59	41	68	84	61	43	72	90	63	34	58	82	57	40	67	78	54
60 and over	15	25	22	17	14	23	28	19	24	40	34	24	16	26	29	20
Unascertained			14				9									

It is evident that the Senate is being affected by the same process as the Dáil : the "Old Guard" in both Houses is dwindling, but it seems that proportionately the Upper House retains more older members than does the Dáil, and the thinning-out has not affected it so noticeably until fairly recently : in 1965, the numbers of veterans were reduced, while in the Dáil the process was obvious in 1961. It would be misleading, perhaps, to identify the "senior senators" with the generation who entered politics through its part in the revolution : the percentage of such senators has tended to be lower than the equivalent in the other House.

---

[3] Dáil Figures : 1944 and 1948, McCracken, *Representative Government in Ireland*; 1961 and 1965, Tuairim Pamphlet No. 15, Senate Figures : See note 2.

TABLE 12:

	1948	1961	1965
% of Senators with revolutionary background	22%	15%	12%
% of Deputies with revolutionary background	43%	19%	10%

Many of the Senate's veterans are men with academic or business backgrounds, who had no connections or only very tenuous connections with the revolutionary movement, or whose connections with it were not so obvious or direct as those of many Dáil deputies. The Senate lives up to the derivation of its name by including comparatively few young men in its ranks; the last election showed some signs that a process of rejuvenation may be beginning; the House seems to have shown few signs of attracting young men entering politics. However, the House of 1965 had a membership which was younger than that of its immediate predecessor.

3. SENATORS BECOMING DAIL DEPUTIES

The opportunity the Senate offers as an entry into Parliamentary politics has, however, increased in another way: the numbers of deputies who were senators immediately prior to their election to the Dáil have increased very markedly: the vast majority of these were "first-time" deputies who had served an apprenticeship in the Upper House.[4]

TABLE 13:

Year Elected to Dáil	1938	1943	1944	1948	1951	1954	1957	1961	1965
Senators who became T.D.s	0	4	4	2	1	1	1	7	5

This reflects more systematised use of the Senate as a "grooming-ground" for the parties: both major parties sponsor this "going downstairs" to the Dáil; in 1961, five of the success-

[4] *Senate Proceedings* 1938-1962.

ful candidates from the Senate were Fine Gael, and two were Fianna Fáil. In 1965, the respective figures were three and two. Occasionally a senator fights a by-election for the Dáil, but successful candidates are rare: in 1960, Senator P. J. Teehan won a seat in the Carlow-Kilkenny by-election, and resigned his seat in the Senate.[5]

4. RETIRED DEPUTIES IN THE SENATE

The Senate has a large core of men in the forty-to-sixty age group, active and well-established in their vocations and in politics; there are indications that the average age of the House is still higher than that of the Dáil, and certainly it contains some veterans who would probably not be able for the faster pace and competitiveness of the Lower House. However, it is a cliché of Irish politics to state that the Senate has a generous complement of retired deputies as distinct from ex-deputies, and it is easy to cite cases: many of them are obvious, the examples among the nominee senators being perhaps particularly so. There seems to be a large vote for defeated deputies available in the Senate electorate: eight of the eighteen ex-deputies in the 1965 Senate had just been defeated at the polls for the Dáil, and about one-third of the panel seats are invariably occupied by people who, at one time or another, were members of Dáil Eireann. In 1943, one-third of the defeated candidates for the Dáil who subsequently stood for the Senate, were elected: the fraction of the remaining candidates who were successful was somewhat less: the bias towards defeated deputies and would-be deputies is slight but discernible. Since the university senators who had held university seats in the Dáils of the Irish Free State retired because of age or died, the university seats have been innocent of ex-deputies. On the other hand, the Taoiseach's eleven has increased its complement of ex-deputies. This is not a phenomenon peculiar to Fianna Fáil Government leaders: a steady increase in the figures for nominee ex-deputies began in 1954 as the table below shows.[6]

---

[5] *Irish Independent*, 25th June, 1960.

[6] Constructed from lists from Newspapers, *Thom's Directories* and Flynn's *Parliamentary Companions*. The method used was to survey the lists of names of deputies in the Dáils since 1919. Care was taken to avoid confusing identities as far as was possible. They check well with incidental statements in Professor McCracken's book and Senator Mullins' quick estimate for the 1957 Senate. After allowing for deaths, I seem to have discovered an extra ex-deputy in that House: see *Senate Debates* 52: 2040-2041, 13th July, 1960.

TABLE 14:

Year	Panels	Ex-deputies in the Senate. Universities	Nominees	Total Senate
1938(1)	12	4	2	18
1938(2)	13	4	2	21
1943	12	3	4	19
1944	10	1	3	14
1948	15	1	2	18
1951	15	1	4	20
1954	13		6	19
1957	16		6	22
1961	15		5	20
1965	12		6	18

Very few of the ex-deputies who win panel seats have vocational nominations: the highest ever figure was four; usually
one or two have such nominations: helping ex-deputies to reach
the Senate is a political party activity almost in its entirety.[7]

TABLE 15:

Year	Ex-deputies on Panel Seats	—With Oireachtas Nomination	—With Vocational Nomination
1938(1)	12	10	2
1938(2)	13	9	4
1943	12	11	1
1944	10	9	1
1948	15	12	3
1951	15	11	4
1954	13	10	3
1957	16	14	2
1961	15	14	1
1965	12	10	2

[7] Table constructed from details of nominations in newspapers. My overall
figures conflict with those given in Report of Committee on the Constitution, 1967, which indicate decline in number of ex-deputies elected to the
Senate.

It is noteworthy that in the 1944 election the number of ex-deputies elected to the Senate reached a record low level, and also that the number increased dramatically in 1948 in the first election under the new Act: this throws some light on the distress of the political parties at the unexplained independence of the voters after the 1944 election!

5. LOCAL COUNCILLORS IN THE SENATE

Between thirty and forty per cent of the members of any particular House have been actively engaged in local government at county or county borough council level at the time they were holding office as senators: twenty of the senators were local councillors in 1944, twenty-five in 1948, twenty-seven in 1951 and twenty-six in 1961.[8] Two of these were nominee senators in 1944 and in 1948, and four were in 1961, so the number on the panels has not varied very much from about one-third of the House, or fifty per cent of the panel members. In 1961, twenty-nine were active councillors or had had experience as councillors, five of these being nominee senators.

Significantly, their strengths on the individual panels are the direct opposite of the strengths of the professional or academically-trained category — that is, there are more of them on the panels on which there tends to be fewer of the others. In 1961 the figures were: twenty-four councillors or ex-councillors held panel seats, nine on the Agricultural panel, seven on the Labour panel, four on the administrative and two each on the Industrial and Commercial and Cultural and Educational panels. Five of these senators had vocational nominations and nineteen had Oireachtas nominations. Labour vocational nominations went to non-councillors, and Administrative nominations went mainly to councillors.

6. OCCUPATIONS OF SENATORS

Trades Unions are, in a way, to the Labour Party in the Senate what local government is to the other two: they nominate candidates to the Labour panel as the local authorities' organisations do to the Administrative panel, and they give them voting appeal. A trade union official has been known to be nominated

---

[8] *Thom's Directory*: lists of Councillors: *Iris Oifigiùil*, 1961, List of Senate electors.

by the Oireachtas Labour party, as Mr Con Desmond was to the Administrative panel in 1961. The Labour party takes care not to make Oireachtas nominations to the Labour panel: they might clash electorally with the Trades Union candidates. In 1948, three of the four trade union officials in the House were Labour panel organisations' nominees: in 1961, three of the six such senators were so nominated. The Senate's Labour Leader is a Trades Union nominee.

As might be expected, the Senate shows a startling variety of occupations, and a variety which is increasing. However, like the Dáil, it has a strong farmers' group, including those who rely on it totally or who combine farming with breeding, shop-keeping, auctioneering or some profession. The Senate tends to have farmers who are the nominees of agricultural societies or interests. The strength of the farming group is roughly equivalent to that of the Dáil, while proportionately it is stronger on the panels than it is in the Dáil. This is connected with the rural bias in the electorate which is spread over the country in proportions more consonant with geographical extent than with actual population figures, unlike the Dáil's constituencies.

The professional category contains a larger proportion of senators than it does of deputies, even when the university senators are excluded, although they account for the bulk of the overall difference. This group has grown in the last twenty years, most of the increase being due to the panels. The panels have doubled their contribution of professionals between 1948 and 1961, the increase being obscured by the decrease in this category among the Taoiseach's eleven.

Unlike the Dáil, the Commercial, Financial and Insurance group has shrunk, although not quite as much as it appears to have in the table below: the 1948 and 1944 figures are inflated by the fact that the Taoiseachs of that time were more inclined to nominate company directors than Mr Lemass was. However, the panels are receiving fewer company directors, shopkeepers, insurance officials and auctioneers than hitherto.

The occupational diversity of the House has grown: professions absent in 1944 and 1948 are evident in the recent Houses, paralleling a similar trend in the Dáil. This is reflected in the fact that the Miscellaneous group, which includes craft workers and trades union officials, has grown: in 1961 the "Others" category included a printer, a painter, a dental mechanic and a foreman.[9]

TABLE 16 :

Year A. Professional	1944		1948		1961		1965	
	Senate	Dáil	Senate	Dáil	Senate	Dáil	Senate	Dáil
Barristers+Solicitors ...	6+1	12+4	4+2	16+7	7+2	13+7	5+2	14+7
Medical Doctors ...	2+1	4+2	2+1	3+2		2+2	1+1	3+1
Teachers	8+2	5	8+1	8	9+2	14+1	10+4	8+1
Journalists	0+1	2+2	2	2	0+2	2	0+2	1+1
Engineers		2+1		2+2	2	2+2	1+2	1+2
Other Professionals ...	1+1		1		1	1+1	2	1+1
Total	17	25	17	31	19	34	19	28
Percentage of House ...	28	18	28	21	32	24	32	19

Year	1944		1948		1961		1965	
B. Commerce, Finance, Insurance	Senate	Dáil	Senate	Dáil	Senate	Dáil	Senate	Dáil
Company Directors ...	4+2	6+4	7+2	8+5	3	12+2	2	13+4
Shopkeepers	4+3	17	3+1	15+2	2+1	11+1	6+1	8+1
Chemists			1	1		1		1
Publicans		1		3	1	6+2	2	7+2
Commercial Travellers		1+1				2		1
Auctioneers	2+2	1+2	2+1	1+3	1+2	4+6	1	3+5
Garage Owners ...					1			1
Estate Managers ...						1		1
Cattle Dealers ...	1+1	1	1+1	1	0+2		1	
Business Managers ...	1				1		1	
Insurance Officials ...	3	1+1	3	1+1	0+1	2+1		1
Total	15	29	17	29	9	39	13	36
Percentage of House ...	25	21	28	20	15	27	22	25

C. Agriculture	Senate	Dáil	Senate	Dáil	Senate	Dáil	Senate	Dáil
Farmers	15+2	39+10	17+2	35+17	15+3	31+14	16+1	34+11
Agricultural Labourers	1							
Total	16	39	17	35	15	31	16	34
Percentage of House ...	27	28	28	25	25	22	27	24

[9] Dáil : Tuairim Pamphlet No. 15.
Senate : Flynn, op. cit., 1945; *Thom's Directory* 1949; *Irish Times*, 7th December, 1961, Professor Chubb's Questionnaire, 1966. There was difficulty in allotting senators of dual occupation, as the Tuairim group also found.

TABLE 16 — *continued*

Year	1944		1948		1961		1965	
D. Miscellaneous	Senate	Dáil	Senate	Dáil	Senate	Dáil	Senate	Dáil
Secretaries of Trade and and other Associations	0+3	1	1+2		0+3	1	0+2	1
Trade Union Officials	5	6	4	6+3	5+2	10	4+1	10
Clerks	1	2	1	3+1	1	1		1
Local Government Employees	1	1+1			1+2		1	1
Building Contractors ...	1	2+1	1		5	1+1		1+1
Bookmakers			1			1		
Others	3	10	2	9	8	6	5	11
Total	11	22	9	25	13	21	9	26
Percentage of House ...	18	16	15	17	22	15	15	18

	1944		1948		1961		1965	
	Senate	Dáil	Senate	Dáil	Senate	Dail	Senate	Dáil
Persons Engaged in Politics		23		27	4	19	3	20
Percentage of House ...		17		18	7	13	5	14

The last category's indication of a sudden jump in the number of professional politicians in the Senate may or may not be very significant: ambiguity in biographical sources may explain it.

The steady growth in the Commercial, Financial and Insurance group in the Dáil, has not, as yet, been reflected in the Senate, or, if it has, it has been kept well under cover. The 1957 Senate was much stronger in this category, having sixteen members who could be loosely classified as businessmen, and an equal number of the professionally employed. In 1961, the Commercial group lost to the Professional group rather suddenly, and it does not occupy the twenty-five per cent or more of the House that it used to, although the 1965 election redressed the balance somewhat. The university members can be relied upon to contribute six university teachers — or an occasional "other teacher" or lawyer in lieu — so that the business group has a greater share than seems evident at first sight.[10] A perspective is provided, however, by the fact that one-third of the second

10 For the 1957 figures, *Senate Debates* 52: 2040-41, 13th July, 1960.

Senate of 1938 could be classified as being in the "Commercial" category. The number of company directors shows a perhaps illusory decline in contrast to the Dáil's figures, and in fact this is the main cause of the decline of the Commercial group. The expansion of the "Miscellaneous-Others" category is certainly an index of the variety of occupations found in the more recent Senates, and it seems to be related to the decline in the number of businessmen and Dublin residents.

7. OCCUPATIONAL STRUCTURE OF THE PANEL GROUP

The occupational structure of the University group is comparatively simple and predictable. It is not worthwhile to try to read any pattern into the occupations of the Taoiseach's nominees. However, it is instructive to note how a "House" of forty-three nominated by such a complicated system and elected by a local authority electorate corresponds to the Dáil — how democratic representation by proportional representation compares with democratic representation at one remove modified to ensure variety in occupations. The figures are derived from the last table.[11] The percentages for the Dáil are given in brackets after the percentages of the group of forty-three.

TABLE 17:

		1948	1961
A. Professional	Barristers+Solicitors	2+1	5+1
	Teachers	3+1	5+2
	Others		2+3
	Total	5	10
	Percentages	12(21)	23(24)

		1948	1961
B. Commercial, Financial Insurance	Company Directors	4+2	3
	Shopkeepers	3+1	2+1
	Others	7+2	2+4
	Total	14	7
	Percentages	32(20)	16(27)

		1948	1961
C. Agriculture	Farmers	15	13+3
	Total	15	13
	Percentages	35(25)	30(22)

[11] Or rather from the Lists from which the last table was derived; see footnote 9.

TABLE 17 — *continued*

D. Miscellaneous	TV Officials	4	5+2
	Others	5+2	6+3
	Total	9	11
	Percentages	21(17)	26(15)

| E. Politics | Persons Engaged in Politics ... | — | — |
| | Percentages ... ... | —(18) | —(13) |

There has been a large change in the occupational structure of the panel seats that has not been reflected in the Dáil. The reasons for this are obscure, but it does seem that the Senate is used by the parties as a place where their more professionally-inclined executives, lawyers and academics may be put, where they can contribute to legislative business even though they are unwilling to sacrifice an active professional career so as to take up the full-time occupation of holding a seat in the Dáil. A Senate seat can, in fact, help the furtherance of a mainly non-political career, through the prominence and influence it gives. It is probably also true that some senators are helped to win their seats so that their remuneration there

. . . . may ease the drain on the party exchequer or on the financial resources of the nominating body.[12]

8. WHERE SENATORS RESIDE

Normally under half of the House is resident in Dublin county, county borough or in the borough of Dun Laoghaire. The figures have remained more or less static since the foundation of the House. University senators normally live in or near Dublin and, in recent years, an increasing proportion of the Taoiseach's nominees tend to be resident there also. Despite the fact that the electorate is heavily biased against the area of Dublin City and County, however, until recently a disproportionate number of panel senators were residents of areas in or around the capital. More panel senators have come from rural areas in recent years, the proportion of panel senators coming from the Dublin area as defined above showing a striking decline from one-third of the House in 1948 to under one-sixth in 1965. It must be remembered that many senators who in the past were

12 *Irish Times*, July 19th 1951, Letter to the Editor.

resident in Dublin had strong rural ties, these being more obvious and perhaps stronger in 1948 than in 1965. Many senators use Dublin residences of friends or relatives for postal purposes or as *pieds-à-terre* in the capital : even so, the shift is a striking one.[13]

TABLE 18 :

Year	Senators resident in Dublin County, County Borough or Borough of Dun Laoghaire		Senators resident elsewhere in Ireland	
	House	Panels	House	Panels
1938(1)	23	11	37	32
1938(2)	27	14	33	29
1943	32	20	28	23
1944	26	13	34	30
1948	26	16	34	27
1951	25	16	35	27
1954	26	12	34	31
1957	24	14	36	29
1961	22	12	38	31
1965	21	9	39	34

9. CONCLUSIONS

It is possible, then, to make a few generalisations. Senators, like deputies, are usually politicians, but hardly of the same type. More of them are professional men, absorbed more in their other occupations than by their lives as public representatives in the Oireachtas : unlike deputies, many senators are not front-rank party men; rather, they are party back-room boys, policy designers, influential backers and organisation workers, and some of them are veterans or even "hacks". There are many "hacks", but not so many as we are sometimes told, and their numbers seem to have diminished since the generation of the revolution started to leave politics and more was being demanded of senators than hitherto. The senators may be tending, like deputies, to become local party representatives and to take up the duties of liaison officer between the State and the public. The Senate may be used by various organisations as a *quid pro quo*, but it is not always the loser by it. While the House has not got the reserve of younger men who are taking over the Dáil gradually, it does have a sizeable complement of knowledge-able members who are capable of contributing usefully to

---

[13] *Thom's Directory;* relevant years, and Flynn, op. cit.

legislative business. Vocational influence reflects itself in speeches, in amendation and, occasionally, perhaps, in divisions : some senators think as much from their vocational viewpoint and experience as they do from their political allegiance : the position in the Dáil is noticeably more partisan, the speeches more committed to a point of view, the atmosphere less leisurely and objective and there is a greater tendency to "play to the gallery". Admittedly, the reason senators play less to the gallery may be that there is less of a gallery to play to : however, this has its benefits. Whether this objectivity and non-partisan attitude stems from the fact that the Senate's functions are less important or from differences in composition is very difficult to say, but it does seem that the emphasised profes-sionalisation—the word vocationalisation is avoided advisedly —of the House has a definite effect on its approach to Parlia-mentary business. The House is a party political assembly, and any vocationalistic characteristics it exhibits seem to be due less to its sophisticated electoral system than to its part-time character.

The non-partisan character of much of the debating is intensi-fied by the eloquently independent contributions of some of the university senators, who contribute a disproportionate amount to the debates : only the party leaders influence the House as much, and they do not, or do not need to, exercise as much control over debate as the Government has to do in the Dáil.

Senators, then, are drawn from similar groups in society as the members of the Lower House : there is not any great social or economic gap between senators or deputies : in fact, in the case of most of them, there is no gap at all. Exceptions are some of the University senators—especially those from Trinity College—and the concession the Taoiseach usually makes to minor groups in his nominations. However, just as the station in life does much to define the man, so does the Senate's func-tions do much to define the senator. He is political, a member of the Oireachtas "club", and he brings his party's point of view to bear on everything that comes before the House as well as his own point of view as an individual. His comprehension of what the provisions of a Bill entail is likely to be higher than that of most of the hard-pressed back-bench Dáil deputies, he has more time to examine legislation and works within a com-paratively non-partisan framework : when it comes to a division, however, he votes on party lines. He is not likely to be a senator unless either his profession makes it convenient in time and in travel, or his political ambitions stretch beyond the Senate and he visualises using it either as a road elsewhere or as an invaluable aid in another direction. Of course, he may well be "retired" and look upon it as a source of a pension or as a pastime. Most senators fit into one or another of these categories.

Chapter Six

MOVES TOWARDS REFORM

1. PUBLIC CRITICISM OF THE CONSTITUTION OF THE SENATE SINCE 1947

While the 1947 and 1954 Electoral Acts met the gravest objections to the electoral mechanics of the House, they did not meet the fundamental criticisms — i.e. that the House had no well-defined function, that the electorate was unsuited to the intended composition of the House as suggested by the categories listed in the Constitution and that the very concept of indirect election was anti-democratic. Neither did they stifle rumours of political corruption completely. Probably inevitably, nobody was satisfied: after the 1954 Senate election, the Association of Municipal Authorities criticised the *reformed* electoral system, and sent a delegation to the Minister for Local Government. They complained also that only one of their four candidates had been successful.[1]

The *Irish Times* and the *Irish Independent* criticised the House, its personnel and its electoral system unfavourably, reserving their sharpest criticism for the nominees of Fianna Fáil Taoiseachs. The comments of these papers on Mr Costello's nominees of 1954 were, however, muted by comparison.[2, 3]

The House was a target for criticism from other quarters as well, however. Following on the formation of the second Inter-Party Government in 1954, the Listowel Cumann of Fianna Fáil resolved that it considered

> . . . that the Senate, as at present constituted, should be abolished and should be replaced by a Chamber elected on a wider franchise and more representative of vocational interests.[4]

[1] *Irish Times*, July 30th and September 23rd, 1954. Another example, *Ibid.*, March 2nd, 1948.
[2] Examples are *Irish Times* 1st August, 1951; 20th July, 1954; 2nd December, 1961 and 19th May, 1965.
[3] *Irish Independent*, 11th December, 1961.
[4] *Irish Times*, 5th October, 1954: Agenda for Fianna Fáil Árd Fheish.

Professor Basil Chubb noted that it was

... one of the platitudes of Irish political life that the Senate is not, and never has been, a body representative of vocational interests, and that it is, on the contrary, composed primarily of party men and dominated by party considerations.

He suggested that the constitution of the House suffered from attempting to achieve two incompatible aims, and that the 1947 and 1954 Acts had merely improved the mechanics of the system, while leaving untouched the dichotomy existing between the principles of party control and vocational representation.[5]

Fine Gael had eloquently criticised the House when it was being set up, and it appears that the second Inter-Party Government were considering possibilities of reforming it. The sudden fall of the Government made any such plans still-born.[6]

The leader of Clann na Poblachta, Mr MacBride, expressed the view in 1954 that the House should be made either democratic or vocational, and called for serious examination of the question whether there was any necessity for its existence.[7] Mr Ralph Sutton commented a few years later, when new official moves toward reform had been made known—

The system we have provided . . . is, perhaps, the best that can be devised in a young Republic : if it had ever been given a chance to operate, it might have reflected great credit on those who devised it.[8]

The nominating bodies have not been happy with the Senate either. Many of them have been reluctant to exercise their rights of nomination at all, preferring to avoid possible political entanglement rather than possess a rather small chance of having a representative in the House.[9] In 1959, the Seanad Nominating Bodies Standing Committee, speaking for nineteen registered bodies, stated in evidence to the Seanad Electoral Law Commission that, while they considered the electorate acceptable, they felt that the Oireachtas should not have the right to nominate candidates. Most of the nominating bodies expressed to the Commission their dissatisfaction with the degree of vocationalisation afforded. Some asked for direct election rights, while one body felt that the facilities afforded to candidates for communicating with the electorate were

[5] B. Chubb: "Vocational Representation in the Irish Senate", *Political Studies*, vol. (ii) 1954, pp. 97-111.
[6] *Dáil Debates* 164:1147, 2nd November, 1957: Mr P. O'Donnell.
[7] *Irish Times*, July 7th, 1954.
[8] R. Sutton, *op. cit.*
[9] Private oral source.

unequal. The Association of Municipal Authorities asked that they be given the right to elect three senators directly.[10]

2. THE INITIATIVE OF DR BROWNE

Dr Noel Browne, then, had considerable potential support from diverse quarters when he moved in the Dáil in November 1957

> . . . that Seanad Eireann as it is at present constituted should be abolished.[11]

Dr Browne argued that the idea that a privileged assembly of people should have an opportunity to reconsider legislative proposals when they had already been through the winnowing processes of the political parties, the press, the civil service, the Government and the Dáil was an impertinent one and repugnant to the democratic ideal. Even in time of crisis, it had no function. It was in the interests of the whole idea of democracy and of democratic Government that

> . . . the pernicious, corroded devitalising influence of the Seanad and in particular of the Seanad election process, should be removed from the arena of public life in this country . . . the Seanad is an expensive pet to maintain.

Dr Browne's frontal assault was blunted somewhat by Mr O'Donnell (Fine Gael), ex-Minister for Local Government in the Inter-Party Government, who moved an amendment urging Senate reform rather than abolition.[12]

The Taoiseach, Mr de Valera, expressed sympathy with the idea of direct vocational representation, but felt that the country was not ripe enough for it yet.[13] He felt that the Fine Gael amendment should be accepted and that a new commission be set up to propose reform within the present framework of the panel system as enshrined in the Constitution.

3. THE REPORT OF THE SEANAD ELECTORAL LAW COMMISSION

A Commission on the Seanad Electoral Law was set up on 28th May, 1958; it reported less than a year later, and its Report was made public at what was possibly an appropriate moment, but was certainly an inopportune one: the Senate had just rejected the Third Amendment of the Constitution Bill, 1959.

---

[10] Seanad Electoral Law Commission: *Summary of Evidence*, Appendix I of *Report*.
[11] *Dáil Debates* 164:835, 1131 and 1456: 27th November to 4th December, 1957.
[12] *Ibid.* 1155 *et seq.*
[13] *Ibid.* 1455 *et seq.*

This important proposal to abolish the method of proportional representation in elections to office in the State had been backed very strongly by the Government, and this was the first time that a capacity vote in the Senate had been hostile to the Government since the House was first constituted in 1937. As has been described earlier, the results of the critical divisions were due to the illnesses of two Government supporters and to the hostility of all six university senators to the proposal. Even a "tie" vote might have saved the Bill, despite an alleged convention that the Cathaoirleach's vote should be such as to ensure reconsideration of the whole matter. The unexpected abstention of a vocational senator dashed any hopes the Government might have had of that happening. Another vocational member voted against the Bill. The Opposition and the *Irish Times* were jubilant.[14]

Fianna Fáil reaction was mixed, ranging from resignation to annoyance.[15]

Twenty-one people were appointed to the Seanad Electoral Law Commission which reported at this juncture. Six were Dáil deputies, one an ex-deputy, while four were senators and one an ex-senator. The political sympathies of eight were Fianna Fáil, of five Fine Gael and of two Labour. Two were politically independent, while the sympathies of the remaining four were doubtful. It would seem that active participation in party politics was a better guide to their attitude toward reform than the nature of their political allegiances.[16] In fact, thirteen were actively engaged in politics, and the remaining eight were surprised at the extent to which these agreed with each other.[17]

The Commission decided to recommend vocationalisation of the House, and argument centred mainly on the number of seats to be allocated to the vocational bodies for direct election.[18] Views as to the most desirable method of election were diverse.[19] Two reservations were recorded—Major Vivion de Valera, S.C. expressed his doubts as to the desirability of mixing vocationalism and politics, while Mr Corish expressed dissatisfaction with the vocational idea and questioned the necessity of a Second Chamber. He declined to sign the Report.

---

[14] *Irish Times*, 30th April, 1959.
[15] *Ibid*. 30th April, 1959.
[16] Private oral source.
[17] Senator Michael Hayes: *Senate Debates* 52:665, 20th January, 1960.
[18] Private oral source.
[19] *Seanad Electoral Law Commission: Report*, 1959.

Otherwise, agreement was unanimous, but only at the cost of much compromise. Signatories from both major parties later expressed their distrust of its conclusions.[20]

The Report described the House's duties as being political, and suggested that its composition would have to take account of this fact. The present system, it observed, permitted people "whose interests could be regarded as party political rather than vocational" to be elected to the panels. However the Commission felt impressed with the arguments in favour of vocationalism, and also with the idea that a continuity in composition and experience would benefit the House.[21] Its recommendations, in view of these conclusions, would be an attempt to reconcile the "two principles" embodied in the Chamber's constitution.

The changes it recommended were not to be a final solution, but were envisaged as a step toward putting the composition of the House on such a footing that it would be made up of persons "of distinction, if not eminence" in their own walks of life.[22]

The Report proposed a scheme whereby the panel system would be converted so that one half of the panel members would be completely vocational, and the remainder would be political. A return to the system of fixed numbers of seats on each sub-panel for vocationally and politically nominated candidates was advocated. In the scheme, twenty-three of the forty-three panel seats were reserved for nominating bodies' nominees:

TABLE 19:

Panel	Present minimum Allocations of Seats on *each* sub-Panel	Proposed Oireachtas sub-Panel	Proposed Nominating Bodies' sub-Panel
Cultural and Educational	2	2	3
Labour	4	5	6
Agricultural	4	5	6
Industrial and Commercial	3	4	5
Administrative	3	4	3
Totals	16	20	23

[20] *Senate Debates* 52:664 and 2031.
[21] *Seanad Electoral Law Commission: Report*, 1959, p. 15.
[22] *Ibid.*, p. 23.

The nominations permissible to the vocational sub-panel were to be restricted by a complicated formula similar to that actually in use since 1954. However, a new feature of the scheme was the proposal that there be separate ballot-papers for each sub-panel.

By having each body registered for a vocational sub-panel appoint five or more electors, the electorate for each sub-panel would be at least 100. These would be entitled to vote only for candidates on the relevant nominating bodies' sub-panel. If the number of bodies registered for a sub-panel was less than three, it was recommended that

> . . . the electorate should be formed on a pro-rata basis of the membership represented by the registered bodies provided that where only two bodies are registered neither body shall have a lesser number of electors than the quota sufficient to secure a candidate.

Further, if the bodies fulfilled the requirements of a Board of Assessors, they would be permitted to elect senators directly on to their sub-panels with no intervening electorate. The Oireachtas sub-panel electorate would remain unchanged. The Board of Assessors' function would be to examine the qualifications of candidates for nomination and of the nominating bodies for registration and to revise the registers annually; its decisions would be final. Its membership would consist of the Ceann Comhairle of the Dáil and nine other members, two each from the Dáil and the Senate and one to be appointed or elected by each vocational sub-panel's Electoral College of nominating bodies. The Ceann Comhairle would be Chairman of the Board and would have a casting vote only.

It would be mandatory, instead of discretionary as it is in practice, for the registering authority to disqualify a body which did not conform to the present requirements concerning Annual General Meetings procedure, business and audit of accounts and revenue, and which, in addition, had not been in existence for at least three years prior to registration, possessed a membership of at least 250 and did not possess a roll of members open to members' inspection. However, bodies representative of large sections of the community, especially bodies which were essentially federations of smaller organisations, would be exempted from these requirements.

Casual vacancies would, on the Oireachtas sub-panels, be filled in the present manner. On the others, the same suggested system of election would be used, nomination would be as at present, and, if the vacancy were in a seat subject to direct election, the by-election would also be direct.

The Report, in conclusion recommended that, after a trial period, the scheme be re-examined to ascertain whether a further advance on these lines was desirable.

The scheme was, in sum, an attempt to follow the tradition envisaged by Mr de Valera in 1937 : it was vocational and it was a logical development of the existing scheme in a particular direction.   More questionable is the assumption that the scheme propounded was, in fact, a method of escaping from the dilemma of a Second Chamber which is expected to be both political and apolitical at the same time.   The political acceptability of the scheme was marginal, however, and it was unlikely that any Government valuing its control over the mechanism of State would be willing to put it into operation in its entirety.

Even the Commission itself had had doubts about the variability of the quotas involved in the scheme, and there were suggestions that the electorate might be expanded in some way to build up the quotas, but the Report did not describe the suggestions.   Had the system been used for the 1957 Seanad General Election, the quotas might have been as follows[23] :

TABLE 20 :

Panel	Quota for Oireachtas sub-Panel	Quota for Nominating Bodies' sub-Panel
Cultural and Educational	291	26
Labour	146	15
Agricultural	146	15
Industrial and Commercial	175	17
Administrative	175	26

The quotas involved for the vocational sub-panels certainly seemed small and not very attractive in view of experience of the 1937 Seanad Electoral Act.

Party leaders on both sides of the Dáil must have viewed the

23 *Ibid.*, p. 19 Scheme described pp. 17-19, 20 and 21.

scheme with unease: under the present system, the major parties can count on a certain minimum number of panel seats, but in the Commission's system, only twenty seats were allotted to the local councils, and Fianna Fáil could, perhaps, have counted on winning ten or eleven of these seats had the system been used in 1961. Vocational bodies would have had to be depended upon to supply nine or ten more seats so that the Government would have an acquiescent Senate. Furthermore, the electorate for these seats would be comparatively immune to propaganda, influence or organisation. It must also be remembered that the Government had just had an example of how independent university or vocational senators could be. The party organisations' penetration of the bodies' electorate would be very partial and unreliable for a while at least, and to achieve complete control would be difficult, although the parties would inevitably be tempted to try. The consequences of a drive by all the parties to "capture" vocational organisations would be incalculable, and might engender totalitarian visions. The end of improving the Second Chamber hardly seemed worth the means required. On the other hand, if bodies were to obtain the right of direct election, their control of political power in the form of Senate seats would be unpalatable to all political parties and, ultimately, to the general public, if they succeeded in acquiring the balance of power in the Chamber. Furthermore, the gain in expertise and talent for the House was not guaranteed.

The Report failed to come to grips with the central problem of defining the purposes for which a Second Chamber was required in the Irish context. This was not really the commission's fault, as its terms of reference precluded a critical examination of the constitutional provisions themselves: in other words, it had to assume a panel system, an electoral system and a necessarily complicated mechanism of registration, nomination and election or selection.

4. THE FATE OF THE REPORT

The Commission reported on 28th March 1969. Queries by Dr Browne[24], Mr Corish and other deputies[25] as to whether the Government intended to implement the proposals were answered

---

24 *Dáil Debates* 174:45, 8th April, 1959.
25 *Dáil Debates* 176:1186, 15th July, 1959, 177:293, 22nd October 1959 and 178:592, 26th November, 1959. The quotation following is from the last citation.

in a non-committal fashion, and the Minister for Local Government expressed a wish to have the matter discussed by the public and by the Senate itself before any action was undertaken.[26]

On 17th February 1960, the Senate debated the motion, proposed by Professor Stanford of Trinity College

> that Seanad Éireann is of opinion that the Government should introduce legislation to implement the recommendations of the Seanad Electoral Law Commission.[27]

The debate centred around the basic recommendation—that twenty-three panel senators be both nominated and elected by the vocational bodies independently of the Oireachtas and of the local government councils.

The Commission's proposals were fully endorsed by only two of the speakers, and one of these was Senator Sheridan, who had remained neutral on the P.R. issue in 1959. Most of the speakers were unenthusiastic about the proposals. The debate was hardly remarkable for its objectivity: of those supporting vocationalisation, only one was an Oireachtas-nominated senator, while only one vocationally-nominated senator actually supported the status quo. The Minister for Local Government, in replying to the debate, argued that vocationalisation would ultimately mean that the senators would become habitually abstentionist whenever political affairs were under discussion. The bulk of the House would have no overriding Parliamentary loyalty but would be guided mainly by the special interests which they represented. Their participation in political life would be sporadic and not particularly relevant or desirable. He criticised the rather small quotas involved in the Commission's scheme, remarking that the size of the quotas had been the downfall of the pre-1948 electoral system. Six weeks after the Senate debate — which was not well publicised — the Commission's scheme was rejected on the grounds that it was neither desirable nor possible to exclude politics from the Senate and that in any case, the proposed reforms would not make much difference.[29] Later it was stated officially that the existing system would be used *faute de mieux* until someone had a better idea.[30] It would seem that many people, in official circles and

---

26 *Dáil Debates* 178:1278, 10th December, 1959.
27 *Senate Debates* 52:623 et seq. 17th February, 1960: resumed 52:2031, 13th July, 1960 and concluded.
28 *Ibid.*, 52:631.
29 *Irish Times*, 29th August, 1960.
30 *Dáil Debates*, 193: 14th March, 1962, col. 1512.

elsewhere, were heartily tired of the Senate and would have liked to drop the subject.[31] Various people have discussed the problem of the Senate publicly since then, and articles on the subject have a habit of cropping up regularly.[32]

The all-party Committee on the Constitution which was set up in 1966 devoted some time to the Senate. The *Report,* which was published in December 1967, added very little new to the long rambling debate on bicameralism which has been going on in this country since 1920. In fact, it echoed the remarks made in 1961 by the Minister for Local Government:

> . . . . the duties of the Seanad are political and the decisions which it is required to take will always be political no matter how it is composed. *The purpose of the Seanad is to deal with the affairs of the community as a whole and not to look after the interests of any special groups or associations.* (my emphasis)

At the same time, the *Report* recommended that the vocational principle be retained, and even be intensified, presumably on the lines suggested by the Seanad Electoral Law Commission. (P.31). No breaking away from the representative principle was contemplated by the Committee. In effect, the present system was settled for, rather than have to embark on a long, elaborate and possibly useless reexamination of the problem. In the meantime the Senate remains trapped, as it always has been, between its own theory and its own practice, easily criticised and slightly comic: it continues to be

> . . . neither the fish of party nor the flesh of non-party — not even the good red-herring of the House of Lords.[33]

---

[31] *Ibid.,* 192: 6th December, 1961, col. 1292.
[32] For example: Professor Quinlan at University College Cork in *Irish Times,* 16th February, 1965, or V. Browne: "Reform the Dáil", *Business and Finance,* 29th April, 1966, or: articles in *Leargas—Public Affairs* during 1968.
[33] *Irish Times,* 1st August, 1951, Leader.

Chapter Seven

CONCLUSIONS

1. THE ROLE OF THE SECOND CHAMBER

In federal states the Upper House has an easily defined role: it provides representation for the units of the federation, while the Lower House, as in unitary states, provides popular representation. The division of powers is often coordinate, the Lower House becoming more predominant as the federal provinces or states are accorded less autonomy, and neither House is genuinely predominant if there is any genuine degree of federalisation. As democratic theory and practice normally sites all representative authority in the Lower House in unitary states, there can be no such clear-cut representative function to impart such authority to a Second Chamber. Its represenative function becomes even less clear-cut if there is no constitutionally recognised aristocracy of wealth, authority or blood in the state whose interests need, or are believed to need, the protection which a suitably constructed Upper House might afford.

Conversely, if a Second House is required for reasons other than representative ones, the problem arises as to what alternative basis of representation should be used to determine its composition; in fact it has to be decided whether a representative basis is required at all. In sum, such a Chamber, if it is to exist in a unitary state like Ireland, must have functions other than representation if it is not to be an absurdity, even if it does include a representative element in its make-up as a subordinate feature of its *raison d'etre*.

The Irish example represents a unique attempt to overcome this problem and it reflects many characteristics of an experiment which was abandoned half-way. It can reasonably be argued that the two functions it was called upon to fulfil are not both being fulfilled: either it is not contributing to legislation, or it is not representing. On the available evidence, it falls down on the latter function, basically because the class or stratum which it was intended to represent is undefinable: it exists, but it is not a coherent group; rather it is a medley of groups culled from different sections of Irish society, with few interests in common and liable to take particularist lines on national issues: in this sense, vocationalism is the direct and irreconcilable opponent of political activity: in fact, politics in our sort of society exists to soften the clash of vocational interests. As Government spokesmen have, in effect, pointed out, an assembly of vocationalists would resemble a Parliament consisting solely of Nazis and Communists.

The intangible character of the concept of vocationalism has also meant that even a determined attempt to create a vocational assembly would fall down: even if it were successful, the resulting assembly would soon find that its "constituencies" were out of date, as sectional interests changed their characteristics, different alignments grew up between them and splits and secession movements developed in accordance with the development of the Irish economy, the changes in the pattern of Irish society and, possibly, in the character of Irish political life. To attempt to enshrine such an inchoate group of forces in legal phraseology does not seem feasible, or even desirable. As the structure is informal, the institutions cannot, through formalism, wilfully ignore that informality.

By and large, the House is reasonably well fitted to fulfill its major role of contributing to legislation, even though, in effect, it supplies a second tier of polticians through which legislation must be passed. The undeniable success of the House of Lords in recent years challenges the assumption that any extraordinarily specialised type of legislator is required for such a task.

Of course, the House of Lords is not directly comparable: in a large unitary state like the United Kingdom, where an industrialised and complex society requires a large volume of legislative activity, there is a clear-cut role for a Second Chamber — any Second Chamber. Despite its extraordinary composition, the House of Lords has a definite field in which to prove its worth. It examines legislation sent to it from the Lower House, giving particular attention to the more complicated and specialised type of Bill for which the machinery of the parliamentary drafting office has proved inadequate, and for which the Lower House has not got the time. Bills are not criticised normally with reference to their principles or objectives, but rather with reference to the consequences of the particular way they have been drafted and to ensure that their texts say exactly what they are intended to say : thus the Lord's function is to perceive the administrative consequences of enactments, including orders and regulations made under the provisions of parliamentary statutes.

Secondly, the House has the function of initiating non-controversial Bills, examining them fully and thus permitting a rapid passage through the Commons. Its delaying powers are intended to be used, not in defiance of the Government, but rather to enable the Government to reconsider the possible consequences of a Bill. It also has the non-legislative task of providing a forum for informed and comparatively objective debate on

> . . . not so much great issues of public policy but matters of administration and of the working of social policies for which the Commons seemingly has little time . . . or inclination.[1]

Less than a hundred Lords are, however, kept busy by the volume of work available. With regard to the accepted attitude to legislation and to the power of suspension, Crick remarks

> The presumption is now, at least amongst Labour and Liberal constitutional writers, that the Lords or indeed any Second Chamber are not a proper body, to set themselves up as interpreters of the Nation's will over the Commons.[2]

How far is this situation analogous to that of the Irish Senate? The political consensus of the past thirty years seems to have decided that the proper function of the Senate lies in careful and objective revision of legislation, the handling of important but non-controversial Bills, the examination of statutory instruments and the discussion of the administrative implications of Government policy : its true *raison d'etre* is to save time for the representative House, to have work delegated to it by the cabinet and to make a distinctive contribution to legislative business. In this sense at least· the Senate, even if it consisted of nothing but political nominees, should be non-political. A corollary of this is that representative principles would be a means rather than an end if applied to the Second House. Ministers should not be politically responsible to a Senate of this type, but they should be informed by the senators of any unintended consequences their legislation might have.

Very few genuinely uncontroversial Bills do pass through the Oireachtas. In practice, little distinction is made between criticism of ends and criticism of means : in fact, it might be

---

[1] Crick, B.: *The Reform of Parliament* quote from p. 114. On functions of Lords, p. 105 *et seq.* and p. 144 *et seq.*
[2] *Ibid.*, p. 107.

said that in the last decade, criticism of means has virtually replaced criticism of ends in Irish political life. This "death of ideology" has caused a blurring of the distinction between formulation and implementation of policy, and seems to be the seminal cause of Mr Lemass's criticisms of the Senate's activities.[3]

The type of politician who has been attracted to the Senate has changed fundamentally. Semi-retired political veterans, neutral representatives of interest groups or silent receivers of patronage no longer constitute the bulk of members. As the parties' hold over sections of the electorate and over the seats in the House becomes firmer because of increased sophistication in the process of nomination, canvassing and campaigning, the typical senator is liable to have the same desire as a Dáil deputy has to criticise Government policy decisions and to make political capital out of legislative business. Well-informed party men and semi-political academics have changed the House's character, and the residual conservative character imparted to it in its early years by many of its most prominent members has practically disappeared. Between 1957 and 1965 a definite, but rather confused, attempt was made by Opposition groupings to turn the Chamber into a more actively political assembly, to increase its involvement in the mainstream of Irish political life and to reverse the process by which the Executive and the Dáil have become the unrivalled centres of political power and legislative activity.[4, 5] This effort seems to have failed: since the 1965 election, there have been examples of intense partisan debate[6] but the senators have ceased to bemoan their fate.

The political composition of the Senate becomes obvious only in connection with intensely controversial national issues: the more intense the controversy, the more the House tends to resemble the Dáil, and the smaller the original contribution it can offer. The House's habitual objectivity stems from its impotence, not from its composition. It is by no means unsuitable for the role of a revising assembly, and has shown itself capable of acting as such, but any attempt to make it take up a political attitude independent of the Dáil's not only will be crushed by the

---

[3] *Senate Debates* 51:1112, 25th November, 1959 and 56:473, 13th March, 1963.
[4] See *Senate Debates* 52:635, Senator Ó Donnubháin, 17th February, 1960. My personal impression agrees with his.
[5] See, however, *Irish Independent*, 12th January, 1966.
[6] *Senate Debates* 61:781 et seq., 8th June, 1966.

Government but also must necessarily be a denial of the House's only real justification for its existence.

The question then arises as to whether a Second House as elaborately equipped as the Irish example, nearly as large as the active element in the House of Lords, can find enough work to do in a small, unitary state like Ireland.

Two examples from small countries of equivalent dimensions would tend to suggest that it cannot find sufficient work. The abolition of the Second Chamber in New Zealand in 1950 caused no great outcry; its abolition was brought about under a conservative government, but this measure was due more to the personal predilection of the Prime Minister than to any public agitation. Conservative misgivings were allayed by the entrenchment of certain constitutional provisions, although an organised group exists which has the reestablishment of bicameralism as its objective.[7] Public attitudes towards it were, by and large, neutral or cynical, although its Statutory Revision Committee was acknowledged to serve a purpose.[8]

Another analogous situation existed in Denmark after 1930[9]: the Upper House, which was elected for longer terms than the Lower House, opposed the new Social Democratic Government, and the Government proposed that it be abolished. However, by 1937 the Social Democrats had obtained a majority in the Upper House and it was reprieved. The Conservative party grew less enthusiastic about bicameralism once the 'time-lag' began to favour the Left. One wonders what would have been the Fine Gael attitude towards the Second Chamber had a Fianna Fáil dominated Free State Senate survived to preside over the formation of the first Inter-Party Government in 1948: the Danish conservatives were not unaware of a parallel possibility ten years earlier. Plans for a new and more docile *landsting* (Second Chamber) were agreed upon between the parties but were rejected by a popular referendum in 1939. After the war, a unicameral parliament was established.

The first Irish Senate, and the New Zealand Upper House were abolished for very different reasons — the former because of its self-assertiveness, the latter because of its inoffensiveness. The Danish example parallels the Irish one. The present Irish Senate, while not yet as passive as was the New Zealand

---

7 Scott: *the New Zealand Constitution* (1962) pp. 6-7, 20 and 50.
8 Brady: *Democracy in the Dominions* (1962 edition) pp. 285-287.
9 Andrén, N.: *Government and Politics in the Nordic countries* (1964).

Chamber, may err on the side of timorousness at times, but it is walking a very difficult tightrope in attempting to avoid being overshadowed by the Dáil while not arousing the Government's ire.

The House has not succeeded notably in carving out for itself an easily defined niche in the Oireachtas. Probably through inertia rather than by deliberate policy, no tradition has grown up of permitting the Upper House to have the lion's share of that type of legislative business most suited to it. Its revisionary work may be excellent, but the Government has not found its contributions so essential and irreplaceable that it takes care to plan its legislative timetable so that the Senate can always revise effectively, nor do ministers of any party, by and large, seem unduly perturbed when the House is denied the opportunity of careful revision during the "rush" periods of the session. During the weeks at the end of the session in the summer, the Oireachtas becomes virtually unicameral in its treatment of the legislation which has accumulated. The volume of the House's revisionary work has grown, but not enormously, in the quarter century since it was first instituted. Possibly there are prospects of a future growth of this sort. Its delaying power is virtually a dead letter. Its debates, however excellent, often have a slight air of unreality; as they are not as well publicised as the Dáil's, Ministers are not inclined to put their cases as thoroughly and tend to leave that to their allies in the Chamber. Its detachment robs its affairs of a certain immediacy which the Dáil's possess.

The part-time character of the Senate's activities puts a ceiling to the amount of work which it is willing to do: if its weekly timetable were extended considerably it might cease to attract the professional type of member it possesses at present. Increases in the volume of business are usually reflected by the House's sitting late rather than by an increase in the number of sitting days every year: an increase in the volume of work would lead to a further decline in the amount of time it devotes to general debate. Suggestions that a special day be set aside for motions, with a time limit to each speaker, have been made.[10]

2. PROSPECTS

It is, I think, fairly plain that a sizeable alteration in the Senate's status would only be achieved in the context of a radical reshuffle of Irish Parliamentary institutions, and might even

---

[10] Senator Eoin Ryan, orally.

have to await the unlikely eventuality of a redefinition of the relationships between the Executive and Parliament. Until then, it is to be tolerated as being innocuous. In a sense, its situation is best seen as a caricature of the Dáil's situation, both Houses having suffered from a withdrawal of prestige and authority from Parliament into the Cabinet. Of course this tendency is by no means peculiarly Irish, but it does seem that authority in the Irish political system has become very centralised. The causes of this centralisation have not been well-researched. It sems that the size of the country, the absence of large socio-economic interest groupings and the comparative simplicity of Irish political life have had a lot to do with it: it is not true to say that an overweening bureaucratic elite has usurped the functions of the people but rather it seems that the low performance of popular organisations in the past has forced the executive to take the initiative in areas where all agreed private action would have been preferable to State action.[11] The fixation on vocational organisation characteristic of many observers of Irish politics was, of course, directly related to a recognition of this vacuum in Irish life which, hopefully, economic development is starting to fill.

The growing importance of the Government's executive and administrative roles has injured Parliament. This, I think, is undeniable. The decay of the Senate is merely an exaggerated version of the neglect from which Parliament, as a whole, has suffered since the 1920s in this country. Basically, this atrophy stems from the disadvantage the Parliamentary debater is at when he is faced with the expert and well-researched civil service minute as a rival for the Minister's attention.

Thus, it is difficult to discuss Senate reform separately from reform of Parliament in general. The oddness of its electoral system and the contrast between its pretensions and its actual place in political life ensure its eventual reform or abolition. Its hopes of survival lie, I believe, in its being converted into a small assembly possessing negligible political power, but containing in its ranks administrative, judicial, vocational, academic and political expertise, whether selected through electoral mechanism or otherwise. Such a House would derive its power from the prestige of its members rather than from any legal grant. As the representative principle would be irrelevant to

---

[11] See Birch, A. H., *Representative and Responsible Government* (1964) p. 105 *et seq.*

such a House, its personnel might well be determined by some independent body, perhaps on the lines of the Civil Service Commission, the Taoiseach making the final choice from a roster of names drawn up by the authority. Some seats might be elective, but not many: an Administrative chamber does not need elections. Some such scheme would remove the onus which has bedevilled the present Senate — the onus to look like a vocational assembly or at least to behave less like a political assembly. This has led to confusion between functionalism *pre se* and functionalism as a means of supplying experts to Parliament. Again, the attempt to combine political parties and interest groups has tended to obscure the worthwhile work that the Senate does. The 1959 Commission and the 1967 Committee both suffered from this myopia. The vocational idea seems to have been seen in Ireland as a possible way of resolving the political antagonisms generated by the Anglo-Irish treaty. It was always a somewhat utopian idea, and it was usually thought of as a system which could be superimposed on society, rather than as a state of affairs which might evolve naturally as a consequence of the growing complexity and sophistication of Irish life. Mr de Valera's gesture toward these ideas and toward their proponents was not intended to be much more than a gesture, but it had the rather unexpected consequence of rendering the formal and elaborate constitution of the Senate an anomaly in the midst of a natural growth in socio-economic interest groups which has made the 1943 *Report* on Vocational Organisation an historical curiosity. The recent development of functional councils like the NIEC and the NAC has, despite the well-publicised difficulties which these bodies have faced and still face, far greater significance for the growth of functional organisation in Ireland than have the provisions of the Senate's constitution.[12] The French Government has not availed itself much of the services offered by the national "Economic Councils" established under the Fourth and Fifth Republics, mainly because these are constituted as basically Parliamentary bodies and behave as such and not as purely advisory and specialised assemblies.[13]

NIEC, an *ad hoc* body, has, by contrast, acquired a very wide influence on Government economic and social policy, and on

---

[12] See Birch, A. H., *op. cit* p. 113 on this problem; for another view, see Amery, L. S.: *Thoughts on the Constitution* (1947), pp. 64-68.

[13] Wheare, K. C.: *Legislatures* (1963 edition) pp. 217-218.

public opinion. In Ireland, the machinery of collective bargaining works rather creakily, but would hardly be helped by being transferred to a Second Chamber. The formulation of national development plans and the design of economic and social policy are, to an increasing extent, carried out vocationally.

The Senate has been by-passed by these developments because it represents the answer given a generation ago to a problem which has only become clear recently.

Reform of the Senate will have to involve a redefinition of its functions in the light of contemporary political theory which assigns a more modest but more clear-cut part to a Second Chamber in the process of Government. Such a reassessment would ignore the red-herring of vocationalism and would involve constitutional amendment. It would also aim at a simplification of the byzantine intricacies of the House's electoral system. The House has suffered from a surfeit of theory : its task is a practical one, and a utilitarian reappraisal of the place of the Senate must be undertaken without recourse to the confusion of theory and practice which has hobbled useful discussion of the Chamber's rôle in Irish political life almost as much as has the entrenchment of the basic lines of the Chamber's structure in the Constitution.

Even after a generation, the Senate's uses are potential rather than actual : it is not, and never has been, used to capacity. Events suggest that the political parties are as much at a loss as to what to do with it as everyone else seems to be.[14] The public attitude to it is one of amusement, cynicism or apathy, and comment on it is rarely uncritical. To some extent, the whole Oireachtas suffers from the same complaints.

Until a rationalisation is brought about the House must be characterised, as Mr de Valera characterised its predecessor, as being "the vestigial remnant of obsolete constitutional arrangements". The natural evolution of modern Government has made the Executive progressively less prepared to tolerate checks and balances which cannot justify themselves and more liable to regard interference with its wielding of authority as an attack on its position.

Governments in Ireland, as elsewhere, have been called upon to assume responsibility for the management of ever widening sectors of the nation's social and economic affairs. Political debate has moved from the theoretical to the pragmatic, and, once

---

[14] See *Report* of Committee on the Constitution, December, 1967. pp. 26-33.

issues have been decided and apparatus set up for the implementation of those decisions, counter-proposals from "Another
Place" are inevitably regarded as obstructive. In the last
analysis, the fate of the Second Chamber in Ireland has been
as much a symptom of this change as it has been the result of
the constitutional architecture of Mr de Valera.

INDEX

A
Anglo-Irish Treaty, 4, 5, 9, 95.
Association of Municipal Authorities, 78, 80.

B
Blueshirt Movement, 10.
Broadcasting Authority Bill, 1959, 47, 50.
Brosnahan, Seán, 36, 64.
Brown, Wilfred, 28.
Browne, Noel, 80, 85.
Bunreacht na hÉireann (Constitution of Ireland, 1937), 1, 10, 16-21, 26, 78, 80, 96.

C
Ceann Comhairle (Speaker of the Dáil), 20, 83.
Chairman of Senate (Cathaoirleach), 40-42, 64, 81.
Chubb, Basil, 79.
Clann na Poblachta Party, 38, 79.
Clerk of the Senate, 28, 31, 40, 41.
Cole, J. C., 47.
Commissions:
  Commission on Revival of Irish Language, 52.
  Commission on Seanad Electoral Law, 79, 80-85, 95.
  Commission on Second House of the Oireachtas, 11-12, 15-21.
  Commission on Vocational Organisation, 25, 52, 95.
Committees:
  Appeals Committee in 1937 Seanad Electoral Act, 21.
  Appeals Committee in 1947 and 1954 Seanad Electoral Acts, 27-28.
  Committee on the Constitution, 1967, 87, 95.
  Interdepartmental Committee on Seanad Electoral System, 28.
  Joint Committee on the Constitution of Seanad Éireann, 1928, 6-8.

Joint Committee on the Seanad Panel Elections, 1947, 26-27.
Senate Committees, 56-58.
Senate Committee on Procedure and Privileges, 41.
Senate Committee on Statutory Instruments, 57-58.
Seanad Nominating Bodies' Standing Committee, 79.
Seanad Select Committee on the Seanad Electoral (Panel Members) Bill, 1952, 28.
Connolly, James, 7.
Constitution of Ireland, see Bunreacht na hÉireann.
Corish, Brendan, 81, 85.
Cosgrave, William T., 6, 7, 10.
Costello, John A., 78.
Crick, Bernard, 90.
Criminal Justice Bill, 1949, 48.
Cumman na nGaedheal Party, 5, 6, 61.

D
" Dáil Constitution," 5, 11.
Dáil Deputies:
  and Senate, 66-69.
Dáil Éireann:
  and Senate of Irish Free State, 3-13.
  and Senate of Bunreacht na hÉireann, 17-20, 42, 49-50, 53, 62-77.
Denmark, 92.
Desmond, Con, 76.
De Valera, Éamon:
  and Senate of Irish Free State, 2-13, 96.
  on Senate reform, 14, 24, 26, 80, 84, 95, 97.
De Valera, Vivion, 81.
Dillon, James M., 26.
Dooge, James, 64.

F
Fianna Fáil Party:
  and Senate of the Irish Free State, 3-13, 92.

R

Register of Vocational Bodies, 29-30.
Returning Officer for Senate elections, 21, 25, 27-32.
Ryan, Eoin, 64.

S

Sheehy Skeffington, Eoin, 51.
Sheridan, J. D., 36, 86.
Sinn Féin Party, 2.
Southern Unionists, 2, 3, 9.
Stanford, William B., 86.
" Succession Bill ", 1965, 54.
Sutton, Ralph, 79.
Seanad Electoral (Panel Members) Act, 1937, 18, 19, 20, 21-23, 84.
Seanad Electoral (Panel Members) (Bye-Elections) Act, 1940, 22.

Seanad Electoral (Panel Members) Act, 1947, 24, 27-32, 78, 79.
Seanad Electoral (Panel Members) Act, 1954, 24, 27-32, 78, 79.
Senators:
    turnover, 38.
    and Senate sittings, 55, 58-59.
    remuneration, 58-60.
    composition, 64-77.
Sweetman, Gerard, 46.

T

Taoiseach (Prime Minister), 22, 23, 26, 38, 43, 44, 51, 54, 59, 95.
Third Amendment to the Constitution Bill, 1959 (" P.R. Bill "), 36, 42, 51, 80-81.
Trades Union Congress, 20.
Transport (No. 2) Bill, 1964, 46.
Tuairim, 62.